A THOUGHT FOR EACH DAY

LAWRENCE C. GAMBONE

Cover Photo:
Crescent Sails, by Lawrence Gambone

CreateSpace On-Demand Publishing, LLC.
© 2018 By Lawrence C. Gambone
All rights reserved. Published 2018
Printed in the United States of America

96 95 94 93 92 91 90 89   10 9 8 7 6 5

ISBN-13: 978-1721757855

ISBN-10: 1721757856

Other Books by Lawrence C. Gambone

Why Corporations Fail
The Dilution of America (with Louis Gilde)

DEDICATION

To the lifeguards and first responders who saved my life in Hawaii . . . had you not done the right things at the right time in the right way, this book would never have been completed.

CONTENTS

	INTRODUCTION	vi
1	JANUARY	1
2	FEBRUARY	21
3	MARCH	41
4	APRIL	57
5	MAY	79
6	JUNE	107
7	JULY	131
8	AUGUST	161
9	SEPTEMBER	185
10	OCTOBER	207
11	NOVEMBER	231
12	DECEMBER	257
	LEAP YEAR BONUS	283

INTRODUCTION

By Jeff Solber

There are probably hundreds, perhaps thousands, of published books containing inspiring, uplifting, and motivational messages; and every one of them does the job well. However, inspiration and motivation by themselves are not enough. You should learn from the stuff you read; and the learning should be enjoyable.

When Larry invited me to write this preface, I accepted readily because we are friends; and, after reading the first draft of the book, I realized that in this book learning, indeed, is entertaining, motivating, and enjoyable.

This exceptional missive contains not only daily thoughts and sayings by famous personages, but is interspersed throughout with interesting facts and information. It has trivia questions and answers that you can use to impress your friends, and facts about people, places, and events that will broaden your understanding of history, life, and the world around us.

Most importantly, it is easy and fun to read.

In effect, some of the daily "thoughts" contained herein are informative, others are inspirational, and others still will challenge you to think. Most, however, are simply fun; they will make you smile and brighten your day—assisted, of course, by occasional witty interjections from Larry.

And, finally, as you read each daily thought, you will experience a reaction: Inevitably you will grin, chuckle, raise your eyes in disbelief, shake your head sadly, and maybe even groan.

But it is all ok, even if you shake your head sadly and groan. You reacted to what you read, just as I predicted . . .

. . . which means that whether you peruse it judiciously day-by-day or whether you devour it voraciously all in one sitting, you will love this book.

So get going — read, gain knowledge, enrich your life, and above all, enjoy.

Jeffrey N. Solber
December 2018

Lawrence C. Gambone

A THOUGHT FOR EACH DAY

LAWRENCE C. GAMBONE

Lawrence C. Gambone

Lawrence C. Gambone

JANUARY

January

Conventionally, January is thought of as being named after *Janus*, the Roman two-faced god of beginnings and transitions. But, according to various Roman writers, *Juno*, the Roman goddess of marriage and queen of the gods, was the month's tutelary deity.

Actually, January (in Latin, *Ianuarius*) is named after the Latin word for door (*ianua*), since January is the door to the year and an opening to new beginnings.

The original Roman calendar consisted of 10 months totaling 304 days, winter being considered a month-less period of approximately 50 days. Around 713 BCE, King Numa Pompilius, the successor of King Romulus, purportedly added the months of January and February, so that the calendar covered a standard lunar year (354 days).

Although March (*Martius*) was originally the first month in the old Roman calendar, January became the first month of the calendar year under either Numa in 713 BCE or the *Decemvirs*[1] (depending on which Roman writer you choose to follow) about 450 BCE[2].

---

[1] (Latin for "ten men") the *Decemvirs* or *Decemviri* were any of several 10-man commissions established by the Roman Republic.

[2] In contrast, specific calendar years were identified by the names of the two consuls who entered office on May 1 or March 15. This changed to January 1 in 153 BCE.

Thought for Today (January 1)

THE "IT'S A NEW YEAR" DEPARTMENT

"Be at war with your vices, at peace with your neighbors, and let every new year find you a better man." – Benjamin Franklin

"Write it on your heart that every day is the best day in the year." – Ralph Waldo Emerson

"Come, gentlemen, I hope we shall drink down all unkindness." – William Shakespeare

"Cheers to a new year and another chance for us to get it right." – Oprah Winfrey

"New Year - a new chapter, new verse, or just the same old story? Ultimately we write it. The choice is ours." – Alex Morritt

"The attraction of New Year is this: the year changes and in that change we believe that we can change with it. It is far more difficult however to change yourself than turn the calendar to a new page." – R. Joseph Hoffman

"What the new year brings to you will depend a great deal on what you bring to the new year." – Vern McLellan

----

Anything I would want to say has been said already, much better than ever I could say it. So I can express only my sincerest New Year wish for all to prosper in the future. - Lawrence C. Gambone (LCG)

Thought for Today (January 2)

THE "THE WISDOM OF LIFE" DEPARTMENT

"The saddest aspect of life is that science gathers knowledge faster than society gathers wisdom."

- Isaac Asimov

Isaac Asimov was born January 2, 1920, in the town of Petrovichi (pronounced peh-TRUV-ih-chee), then in the Russian Soviet Federated Socialist Republic and now in Russia (czarist Russia no longer existed, while the USSR hadn't formed yet). Asimov is the only author who has published a book in 9 of the 10 Dewey-decimal categories (no book was classified in the 100s, Philosophy). He died April 6, 1992 of heart and kidney failure. - LCG

Thought for Today (January 3)

THE "POLITICAL PROTESTATION" DEPARTMENT

"If I walked on top of water, the headline that afternoon would read: 'President Can't Swim'."

- Lyndon B. Johnson

. . . sometimes, maybe, you just "gotta jump in." - LCG

Thought for Today (January 4)

THE "ENEBRIATE IMBIBERS" DEPARTMENT

Alcohol doesn't make you FAT! It makes you LEAN . . . . against tables, chairs, walls, floors, and ugly people.

Yep, alcohol . . . because no great story ever started with someone eating a salad. - LCG

Thought for Today (January 5)

THE "REALLY, REALLY STUPID SAYINGS" DEPARTMENT

If your ship doesn't come in, swim out to it.

. . . finally, my ship came in. Unfortunately, I was at the airport. - LCG

Thought for Today (January 6)

THE "WHAT'S IN A WORD?" DEPARTMENT

The word "nerd" was coined by Dr. Seuss in, "If I Ran the Zoo," published in 1950.

. . . so, nerds; now you know whom to blame. - LCG

Thought for Today (January 7)

THE "ON THIS DAY IN HISTORY" DEPARTMENT

On January 7, 1610, the Astronomer and Physicist, Galileo Galilei, discovered Io, Europa, and Ganymede, the first three satellites of Jupiter.

Born February 15, 1564 in Pisa, Italy, Galileo Galilei was an Italian Philosopher, Astronomer, and Physicist. He was a central figure in the transition from natural philosophy to modern science and in the transformation of the scientific Renaissance into a scientific revolution. Galilei died January 8, 1642. - LCG

Thought for Today (January 8)

THE "INTERESTING FACTS" DEPARTMENT

World's Oldest National Flag

The name of the Danish flag is the *Dannebrog*, meaning, "the flag of the Danes" or "the red flag."

According to legend, the *Dannebrog* fell from heaven during the battle of Lyndanisse, Estonia in 1219. The first recorded use of the flag appears one hundred years later, making the *Dannebrog* the oldest "unchanged" national flag in the world.

. . . I think of the *Dannebrog* every time a bartender tells me I'm flagged. - LCG

Thought for Today (January 9)

THE "WAS THAT A YEAR OR WHAT?" DEPARTMENT

In 1977, the first Apple computer went on sale, Voyagers I and II were launched, and the movie, "Star Wars," made its debut.

In 1977, New York hunters killed 83,204 deer . . . and 7 hunters. - LCG

Thought for Today (January 10)

THE "A HEAD OF THE GAME" DEPARTMENT

The Greek playwright Aeschylus (525-456 BCE) was killed when an eagle dropped a tortoise on his head.

Aeschylus is the first Greek tragedian whose plays still survive (the others are Sophocles and Euripides), although seven only of his estimated seventy to ninety plays still exist.[3] He is described often as the father of tragedy and historians believe that, most likely, he was the first dramatist to present plays as a trilogy (his *Oresteia* is the only surviving example).

In 490 BCE, Aeschylus and his brother Cynegeirus fought to defend Athens against Darius I's invading Persian army at the Battle of Marathon. Cynegeirus died in the battle, for which his countrymen extolled him as a hero. In 480, Aeschylus was called into military service again,

---

[3] https://en.wikipedia.org/wiki/Aeschylus (accessed 6/17/18)

this time against Xerxes I's invading forces at the Battle of Salamis, and perhaps, too, at the Battle of Plataea in 479 BCE.

At least one of Aeschylus' works was influenced by the Persian invasion of Greece. This play, *The Persians*, is the only extant classical Greek tragedy concerned with current history (very few of that kind were ever written), and it is a useful source of information about that period.

So important was the war to Aeschylus and the Greeks that, upon his death around 456 BCE, his epitaph commemorated his participation in the Greek victory at Marathon rather than his success as a playwright. Nevertheless, Aeschylus's works were so respected by the Athenians that after his death, his were the only tragedies allowed to be restaged in subsequent competitions.

Five hundred years after Aeschylus' death, the Roman writer, Valerius Maximus, wrote that Aeschylus was killed when an eagle dropped a tortoise on his head, mistaking it for a rock suitable for shattering the shell of the reptile. Pliny, in *his Naturalis Historiae* adds that Aeschylus had been staying outdoors to avoid a prophecy that he would be killed by a falling object.

Well, Aeschylus . . . I guess you can say "that's using your head." - LCG

Thought for Today (January 11)

THE "OFFICIALLY UNOFFICIAL" DEPARTMENT

Blessed are the peacemakers; for they shall take flak from both sides.

- Unofficial Motto of the United Nations

"There has never been a good war or a bad peace." - Benjamin Franklin

Thought for Today (January 12)

THE "YOU READ IT ON THE ROAD" DEPARTMENT

BUMPER STICKERS:

> THEY COULDN'T REPAIR MY BRAKES
>
> . . . SO THEY MADE THE HORN LOUDER.

> MY WIFE HAS THE GOOD CAR
>
> . . . And The House, And The Kids . . . .

BUMPER STICKER: Drive like Hell . . . you'll get there! - LCG

Thought for Today (January _

THE "WHATEVER YOU SAY" DEPARTMENT

"I invented the cordless extension cord."

- Steven Wright

"I invented the internet." - Al Gore

Thought for Today (January 14)

THE "WAY TO GO" DEPARTMENT

"I was hoping to be on Easy Street by now, but I missed the off-ramp years ago." - Ed Wallerstein

---

. . . I missed the street altogether . . . . - LCG

Thought for Today (January 15)

THE "POLITICAL POLEMICS" DEPARTMENT

Germans know the truth about politicians. The an word for City Hall is "Rathaus."

- L. C. Gambone

't come up with a better name myself. - LCG

Thought for Today (January 16)

THE "WHAT'S IN A WORD?" DEPARTMENT

"Word Play" (*jeu de mots*) or "double entendre" are words, phrases, or sentences that have two meanings. Here are some examples:

- When fish are in schools, they sometimes take debate.
- A thief stole a calendar and got twelve months.
- When the smog lifts in Los Angeles, U.C.L.A.
- The batteries were given out free of charge.
- A dentist and a manicurist married. They fought tooth and nail.
- A will is a dead giveaway.
- With her marriage, she got a new name and a dr
- A boiled egg is hard to beat.
- When you've seen one shopping center you'v mall.
- Police were called to a Day Care Center; old was resisting a rest.
- Did you hear about the fellow whose cut off? He's all right now.
- A bicycle can't stand alone; it is t
- When a clock is hungry, it goes

- Remember the guy who fell into an upholstery n.. He's fully recovered now.

- He had a photographic memory, which was never developed.

- When she saw her first strands of gray hair, she thought she'd dye.

- Acupuncture is a jab well done. That's the point of it.

- Those who get too big for their pants will be exposed in the end.

I'm retired. I was tired yesterday, and I'm tired again today. - LCG

Thought for Today (January 17)

THE "LESSONS IN LIFE" DEPARTMENT

life has taught us anything, it is not just to wonder it is all about, but to actively engage the natural around us." - Gary Zimmerman

---

h and experience the world. - LCG

Thought for Today (January 18)

THE "ENEBRIATE IMBIBERS" DEPARTMENT

"Only Irish Coffee provides all four essential food groups - alcohol, caffeine, sugar and fat." - Alex Levine

---

... finally, a diet I can live by. - LCG

Thought for Today (January 19)

THE "WHO NEEDS A MARRIAGE COUNCELOR?" DEPARTMENT

"By all means, marry. If you find a good wife, you'll be happy; if not, you'll become a philosopher."

- Socrates (469-399 B

"In Hollywood, brides keep the bouquet and throw away th
- Gr

Thought for Today (January 2

THE "WHAT DO YOU HAVE AGAINST GREED?" DEPARTMENT

"Remember, that which you have now was once among the things you only hoped for." - Epicurus (341-270 BCE)

If you have love and health, you have all you need! - LCG

Thought for Today (January 21)

THE "YOU READ IT ON THE ROAD" DEPARTMENT

BUMPER STICKERS:

HONK IF YOU HATE "HONK"

BUMPER STICKERS.

HONK IF YOU LOVE JESUS

. TEXT WHILE DRIVING IF YOU WANT TO MEET HIM.

\h, and "Honk" if you love peace and quiet. - LCG

Thought for Today (January 22)

THE "WHAT'S FOR LUNCH?" DEPARTMENT

"Never eat more than you can lift." - Miss Piggy

A fan magazine asked Miss Piggy about her favorite role. She replied, "A wonderful seven-grain bun." - LCG

Thought for Today (January 23)

THE "I THINK I'LL THINK ABOUT THIS" DEPARTMENT

"Whether you think you can or whether you think you can't, you're right." – Henry Ford

---

. . . so, what if you can't think? - LCG

Thought for Today (January

THE "WRIGHT IS NEVER WRONG" DEPAR

"All those who believe in psychokinesis, raise

- St

. . . All those who believe I actually work, raise m

Thought for Today (January 2...

THE "ASTRONOMICAL FACTS" DEPARTMENT

Dipping into the Big Dipper . . .

In the constellation Ursa Major, Mizar and Alcor form a naked-eye double star in the handle of the Big Dipper. But, in actuality, Mizar is a quadruple star system and Alcor is a binary star system. Together, the pair form a sextuple system.[4]

The proper motions of Mizar and Alcor show that they move together (both are members of the Ursa Major Moving Group), raising the question of whether they are gravitationally bound. In 2009, it was reported independently by two groups of astronomers (Eric Mamajek et al., and Oppenheimar et al.) that Alcor, a binary consisting of Alcor A and Alcor B (a red dwarf star), most likely is bound gravitationally to Mizar. This brings the full count of stars in this complex system to six.

The whole six-star system is located approximately 83 light-years away from Earth. - LCG

---

[4] https://en.wikipedia.org/wiki/Mizar_and_Alcor (accessed 6/17/18)

Thought for Today (January 26)

THE "WRIGHT IS NEVER WRONG" DEPARTMENT

"Boycott shampoo . . . . Demand the real poo."

– Steven Wright

I asked a number of women which shampoo they preferred. The most common answer was, "Eeeeek! How did you get in here? I'm calling the police!" - LCG

Thought for Today (January 27)

THE "WHAT'S IN A NAME" DEPARTMENT

Woflgang Amadeus Mozart's full name:

Johannes Chrysostomus Wolfgangus Theophilus Mozart

Chrysostomus? . . . . And . . . ah . . . what about "Amadeus?"

Mozart was born January 27, 1756 in Salzburg, Austria. He died in Vienna on December 5, 1791. - LCG

. . . Chrysostomus?? . . . . Really??

Thought for Today (January 28)

THE "THOUGHTS ON LIFE" DEPARTMENT

I try not to think: "Could I be in a better place?" Rather,
I think: "How could I make a place better?"

– Lawrence C. Gambone

"Do not spoil what you have by desiring what you have not."
- Epicurus (341-270 BCE)

Thought for Today (January 29)

THE "WHEN ART THOU, ROMEO" DEPARTMENT

Shakespeare's play, "Romeo and Juliet," was published
officially in early 1597. However, it is believed that it
was performed first on January 29, 1595.

. . . Yo, Romeo! - LCG

. . . Chrysostomus?? . . . . Really??

Thought for Today (January 30)

THE "LIMITING THE LIMITLESS" DEPARTMENT

"The difference between genius and stupidity is that genius has its limits." - Albert Einstein

----

. . . You know, Al, if it weren't for stupid people like me, smart people like you wouldn't look so good. - LCG

Thought for Today (January 31)

THE "I WONDER" DEPARTMENT

(Originally the "Interesting Facts" Department)

If Americans call dinner plates made in America, "China," do the Chinese call plates made in China . . . uh . . . "America" (when company comes for dinner, we use the good America)?

Why Porcelain is Called "China."

The Chinese discovered the process for making porcelain and kept it secret for centuries.[5] According to historical records, the town, Jingdezhen, located in the northeast of Jingxi province, has been making porcelain for over 2000 years. The records show that during the Han Dynasty, Jingdezhen became known as the "town of

---

[5] https://en.wikipedia.org/wiki/Porcelain (accessed 6/17/18)

porcelain." During the Han Dynasty, people in Jingdezhen made "blue pottery with glaze."

After the establishment of a Portuguese trading post on Macao in 1557, the first few examples of Chinese porcelain (as opposed to earthenware) found their way to the courts of Europe. It was appreciated immediately, since it was much finer than any European pottery. Indeed, in English, the early term for Porcelain was "china-ware."

During the 17th century imports of china-ware became much more common, particularly of delicate wares to accommodate Europe's new tea-drinking craze. In 1664, Louis XIV granted privileges to a few French potters to attempt porcelain.

The English, too, were attempting to create "china-ware." Their experiments lead eventually to the development of "artificial porcelain" using powdered glass—with the frequent addition in England of ash from charred bones (beginning the specifically British tradition of bone china). This was known as "soft porcelain."

True porcelain contains two substances known from their Chinese names as "Kaolin" (very fine white clay) and "Petuntse" (Feldspar, a rock). These substances fuse at high temperatures to form a natural glass—porcelain. When the secret was discovered in Europe in the early 18th century, the ingredients were, at first, imported from China. But they can be mined also in Europe, where they are known as china clay and china stone (or feldspar).

The first European-produced true porcelain was made in Dresden by Friederich Boettger in 1709; and the first pieces were sold at the Leipzig Easter Fair in 1710. By 1713, delicate white porcelain was produced in Meissen, Germany.

The process for making true porcelain soon became known throughout Europe, and porcelain-producing factories began springing up in France, England, and Germany. And in English, the term, "China-ware," was shortened eventually to the current, "China."

. . . I guess it's a good thing porcelain wasn't invented in Assyria (yeah, I know; it's a bad joke). - LCG

FEBRUARY

February

February comes from the Roman month *Februarius*, which was named after the Latin term *februum*, meaning *purification*. The Romans celebrated the purification feast, *februa*, on the 15th day of this month.

There were some divergences, however; the word comes actually from the Old French *feverier* (based on the Latin *februarius*, from *februa*). The spelling changed in the 15th century to *feverer*, in association with the Latin root and, eventually, became the modern February.[6]

The original Roman calendar consisted of 304 days grouped within 10 months. Purportedly, around 713 BCE, the semi-mythical successor of Romulus, King Numa Pompilius, added the months of January and February, so that the calendar covered a standard lunar year (354 days).

----

[6] In case you're as confused as I am, the word February originated with Latin, switched to French, went back to Latin, and ended up English (go figure). - LCG

Thought for Today (February 1)

THE "CONSTITUTIONAL AMENDMENT" DEPARTMENT

On February 1, 1865, President Abraham Lincoln signed the proposed 13th amendment to the Constitution of the United States to be ratified by the states.

"Neither slavery nor involuntary servitude, except as a punishment for crime whereof the party shall have been duly convicted, shall exist within the United States, or any place subject to their jurisdiction."

In this case, it was constitutionally correct to correct the constitution.
- LCG

Thought for Today (February 2)

THE "KEEP MOVING ON" DEPARTMENT

"Consider each step forward as a step closer to where you are supposed to be." - Anonymous

----

. . . and consider each step backward as a small divergence from your true path. - LCG

Thought for Today (February 3)

THE "CHOCOLATE REVOLUTION" DEPARTMENT

Researchers do not agree which Mesoamerican culture first domesticated the cacao tree;[7] however, the use of the fermented bean in a drink seems to have arisen in North America (Mexico).[8] A ceramic vessel found at an Olmec archaeological site on the Gulf Coast of Veracruz, Mexico, dates the preparation of Chocolate by pre-Olmec peoples to 1750 BCE. On the Pacific coast of Chiapas, Mexico, a Mokayanan archaeological site provides evidence that dates the use of cacao beverages even earlier to 1900 BCE.

Christopher Columbus encountered the cacao bean on his fourth mission to the Americas on August 15, 1502, when he and his crew seized a large native canoe that proved to contain, among other goods for trade, cacao beans. But, while Columbus took cacao beans with him back to Spain, it made no impact until Spanish friars introduced chocolate to the Spanish court in the late 16th Century.

How the English word "chocolate" came into being is not certain. The most accepted theory is that the word "chocolate" entered the English language from the Spanish language.

---

[7] The Latin name for the cacao tree is, *Theobroma cacao*.

[8] https://en.wikipedia.org/wiki/Chocolate (accessed 6/17/18)

According to this theory, "Chocolate" is derived from the Classical *Nahuatl* (Aztec) word *chocolātl*, which is itself a derivation from the Yucatec Maya word *chokol* meaning hot, and the *Nahuatl* word *atl* meaning water.

Another theory put forth by etymologists is that the origin of the word "chocolate" may be from the purely *Nahuatl* word *xocoatl*, which means, "bitter water."

The craze for chocolate, which was served as a beverage only, spread throughout Europe during the 17th, 18th, and into the 19th centuries. However, processing the cacao bean during that period was slow and laborious.

Innovations were introduced during the industrial revolution in the 19th century that made chocolate both cheaper to produce and more consistent in quality. These innovations introduced the modern era of chocolate. Known as "Dutch cocoa," chocolate became machine-pressed, which was instrumental in the transformation of chocolate to its solid form.

And eventually, with the addition of additives such as milk, nuts, and caramel, chocolate became a universal confection.

. . . My thoughts? I love chocolate. I mean, if it "ain't" chocolate, why waste the time and calories? - LCG

Thought for Today (February 4)

THE "WORDS TO PONDER" DEPARTMENT

"It's how you deal with failure that determines how you achieve success."

– David Feherty

. . . I am a very successful failure. - LCG

Thought for Today (February 5)

THE "WORDS TO LIVE BY (or not)" DEPARTMENT

Today's Proverb:

Those who live by the sword get shot by those who don't.

. . . a bullet is faster than a pen and mightier than a sword. - LCG

Thought for Today (February 6)

THE "INTERESTING FACTS" DEPARTMENT

The "Monopoly" board game was released for sale for the first time on February 6, 1935. The format is based upon the streets of Atlantic City, New Jersey.

Cartoonist F. O. Alexander is credited with creating the following characters: "Go to Jail" Officer Edgar Mallory, Jake the Jailbird, and mascot Milburn Pennybags.

"I think it's wrong that only one company makes the game Monopoly."
— Steven Wright

Thought for Today (February 7)

THE "RAGS TO RAGS" DEPARTMENT

It took years of dedication and hard work, but I managed to raise myself up from the depths of obscurity to become a complete unknown. - Lawrence C. Gambone

---

. . . anything I could add here would be superfluous. - LCG

Thought for Today (February 8)

THE "POLITICANA AMERICANA" DEPARTMENT

"There are two [political] parties: the silly party and the stupid party. I'm too old for the silly party, so I had to join the stupid party." - P. J. O'Rourke

---

I belong to my own political party, the "Stupilly Party." It is both stupid and silly (but not in that order necessarily). - LCG

Thought for Today (February 9)

THE "COMMUNING WITH NATURE" DEPARTMENT

With a seven-foot wingspan, the Philippine Eagle is one of the world's largest . . . and one of the most endangered!

"Runaway logging threatens to wipe out one of the world's largest raptors." - National Geographic

The Philippine Eagle grows to over three-feet in length, has a seven-foot wingspan, and can weigh up to 14 pounds.[9] Though not the heaviest raptor (that distinction is held by the Steller's Sea Eagle and the Harpy Eagle), the Philippine Eagle is the longest eagle with the largest wingspan in the world.

In 2010, the bird was listed officially as "critically endangered," with experts estimating that less than 500 remain in the wild. The Philippine eagle is endemic to the Philippines only and can be found on four major islands: eastern Luzon, Samar, Leyte, and Mindanao. The largest number of eagles reside on Mindanao, with (at the time of this printing) approximately 233 breeding pairs. Only a few pairs are found on Samar, Leyte, and Luzon.

"It is possible that no one has ever described this rare raptor, one of the world's largest, without using the word 'magnificent.'" - Mel White

---

[9] https://en.wikipedia.org/wiki/Philippine_eagle (accessed 6/17/18)

Thought for Today (February 10)

THE "YELL IT LIKE IT IS" DEPARTMENT

"I'm not a tech-savvy parent. I communicate with my children via the old-media format called yelling."

- P. J. O'Rourke

I never yell at my children . . . now that they are bigger and stronger than me. - LCG

Thought for Today (February 11)

THE "FAMOUS BIRTHDAYS" DEPARTMENT

"Our greatest weakness lies in giving up. The most certain way to succeed is always to try just one more time."
– Thomas A. Edison

Thomas A. Edison

Born in Milan, Ohio, Thomas Alva Edison (February 11, 1847 - October 18, 1931), an American inventor and businessman, was instrumental in the development of many devices that influenced life greatly around the world. Edison holds 1,093 US patents, as well as many patents in Europe.

More significant than the number of patents is the widespread impact of his inventions: the electric light was incremental in the establishment of power utilities and sound recording advanced the motion picture industry world-wide.

Dubbed "The Wizard of Menlo Park" (New Jersey), he was one of the first inventors to apply the principles of mass production and large-scale teamwork to the process of invention. Because of that, he is credited with the creation of the first industrial research laboratory.

"To invent, you need a good imagination and a pile of junk."
- Thomas A. Edison

Thought for Today (February 12)

THE "WORDS OF WISDOM" DEPARTMENT

"Empty pockets never held anyone back. Only empty heads and empty hearts can do that."
- Norman Vincent Peale

. . . an empty gas tank can hold you back. - LCG

Thought for Today (February 13)

THE "IS IT A SHOPPING LIST?" DEPARTMENT

The world's oldest traces of writing are the Tărtăria tablets, discovered in Romania in 1961, and estimated to date from 5500 BCE. The meaning of the symbols is unknown, and their nature (and authenticity) has been the subject of much debate.

. . . . Maybe it's a laundry list? - LCG

Thought for Today (February 14)

THE "EXTORTION DAY . . . UH . . . I MEAN VALENTINE'S DAY" DEPARTMENT

According to Wikipedia,[10] the first recorded association of Valentine's Day with romantic love is in *Parlement of Foules* (1382) by Geoffrey Chaucer, who wrote:

"For this was on seynt Volantynys day
Whan euery bryd comyth there to chese his make."

["For this was on St. Valentine's Day, when every bird cometh there to choose his mate."]

This poem was written to honor the first anniversary of the engagement of King Richard II of England to Anne of

---

[10] https://en.wikipedia.org/wiki/Valentine%27s_Day (accessed 6/17/18)

Bohemia (a treaty providing for a marriage was signed on May 2, 1381).

Most assume that Chaucer was referring to February 14 as Valentine's Day; but, mid-February is an unlikely time for birds to be mating in England. However, the date on which spring begins has changed since Chaucer's time because of the more accurate Gregorian calendar, which was introduced in 1582. On the Julian calendar in use in Chaucer's time, February 14 would have fallen on the date now called February 23, a time when some birds have started mating and nesting in England.

People say you cannot live without love . . . uh, personally, I think oxygen is more important. - LCG

Thought for Today (February 15)

THE "WORDS OF WISDUMB" DEPARTMENT

Prepping for a colonoscopy can change your whole perspective on "feeling empty inside." - L. C. Gambone

---

. . . . and it's a pain in the you-know-what. - LCG

Thought for Today (February 16)

THE "INSPIRING WORDS" DEPARTMENT

"Of the four wars in my lifetime, none came about because the U.S. was too strong." - Ronald Reagan

---

Ronald Wilson Reagan (February 6, 1911 - June 5, 2004) served as the 40th President of the United States from 1981 to 1989. Prior to the presidency, he had a long, three-decade career as a Hollywood actor and union leader before serving as the 33rd Governor of California from 1967 to 1975. – LCG

Thought for Today (February 17)

THE "YEP, THAT'S HOLLYWOOD" DEPARTMENT

"I'm a marvelous housekeeper. Every time I leave a man I keep his house." - Zsa Zsa Gabor

---

Zsa Zsa Gabor (February 6, 1917-December 18, 2016) was a Hungarian-American actress and socialite. Her sisters were actresses Eva and Magda Gabor. Zsa Zsa began her stage career in Vienna and was crowned Miss Hungary in 1936. She emigrated from Hungary to the United States in 1941. Zsa Zsa was married nine times. She was divorced seven times, and one marriage was annulled. "All in all — I love being married," she wrote in her autobiography. - LCG

Thought for Today (February 18)

THE "ONCE A PUN A TIME" DEPARTMENT

PUN: The fattest knight at King Arthur's Round Table was Sir Cumference — he had too much pi.

. . . That was two-thirds of a pun: P-U! - LCG

Thought for Today (February 19)

THE "PREPOSTEROUS POLITICAL POLEMICS" DEPARTMENT

Democrats believe Republicans are wrong.

Republicans believe Democrats are wrong.

They're both right . . .

. . . providing conclusive proof that two wrongs CAN make a right.

If Pro is the opposite of Con, then is Progress the opposite of Congress? Of course it is . . . only politicians can be wrong, claim to be right, continue to be wrong, take actions incorrectly, and during the resulting repercussions, claim no responsibility for any of it. - LCG

Thought for Today (February 20)

THE "CELEBRITY BIRTHDAY" DEPARTMENT

"Life is a waste of time and time is a waste of life, so let's get wasted and have the time of our lives."
— Kurt Cobain

Kurt Donald Cobain (February 20, 1967 – April 5, 1994) was an American singer, songwriter, and musician. Born in Aberdeen, Washington, Cobain formed the band Nirvana with Krist Novoselic and Aaron Burckhard in 1987, and established it as part of the Seattle music scene which later became known as grunge.

Cobain struggled with heroin addiction, chronic health problems, and depression. He had difficulty coping with his fame and public image. On April 8, 1994, Cobain was found dead at his home in Seattle; his death was ruled a suicide by a self-inflicted shotgun wound to the head.

Since their debut, Nirvana, with Cobain as a songwriter, sold over 25 million albums in the U.S., and over 75 million worldwide. In 2014, Cobain was inducted posthumously into the Rock and Roll Hall of Fame along with Nirvana band members Dave Grohl and Novoselic.

. . . A life composed of so much pain, so much anguish . . . so much talent. - LCG

Thought for Today (February 21)

THE "AMERICANA" DEPARTMENT

"Oh, give me a home,
Where the buffalo roam,
And the deer and the antelope play . . . ."

Dr. Brewster Higley (while inebriated, purportedly) wrote those iconic words back in 1876; and Americans have sung the song ever since. The problem, however, is that, factually, the song is incorrect . . .

. . . you see, there are no antelope in North America.

Commonly called the "American Antelope," the pronghorn ranges throughout the American West. It is the second fastest animal in the world, reaching speeds of nearly 60 mph. Only Africa's cheetah is faster; but, unlike the short-winded cheetah, which can maintain its speed for a few hundred yards only, the pronghorn can maintain a speed of approximately 30 mph over long distances.

Nevertheless, getting back to Dr. Higley's song, here is where the problem arises: According to the Smithsonian's Natural History Museum, the "American Antelope" is not an antelope. The museum's website states:

> *Pronghorns are placed in their own family, the* Antilocapridae, *to distinguish them from antelopes (Family* Bovidae*) or deer (Family* Cervidae*).*

The San Diego Zoo's website states:

> *The pronghorn is an original Native American. It has no close relative on this or any other continent . . . . The pronghorn is often called an antelope, and it does look like many antelope species. Yet it is different enough to warrant its own taxonomic family,* Antilocapridae.

In effect, although there is a physical resemblance, true antelopes are related more closely to cows than to pronghorns, while pronghorns are related more closely to . . . well . . . nothing actually.

The "American Antelope" is unique. It is the sole member of its family (the classification above genera, which is the classification above species).

– Lawrence C. Gambone

. . . More to come. - LCG

Thought for Today (February 22)

THE "AMERICANA 2" DEPARTMENT

"Oh, give me a home,
Where the buffalo roam,
And the deer and the antelope play . . . ."

We know now that Dr. Higley was wrong about the antelope. But, unfortunately, it doesn't end there. In fact, actually, it gets worse! Higley really got it wrong because . . . are you ready for this?

. . . . There are no "buffalo" in North America.

The American "buffalo" are not buffalo; they are bison (the only true buffalo are the Asian water buffalo and the African cape buffalo). The North American hoofed mammals that, for many people, embody the American West, are often referred to as buffalo; but even though they are classified as *Bovidae*, which is the same family group as Old World buffalo species, American bison are not related closely to those species. Rather they are related more closely to the European Bison, making the common name "buffalo" misleading.

– Lawrence C. Gambone

Ok, now you have some grand trivia questions. Ask your friends if there are antelope and buffalo in America, amaze them with the true answer, and recommend that they purchase this book to obtain the source of your information. - LCG

Thought for Today (February 23)

THE "AMERICANA 3" DEPARTMENT

"Oh, give me a home,
Where the buffalo roam,
And the deer and the antelope play . . . ."

Well, on the bright side, Dr. Higley was right, at least, about the deer. There are deer (family *Cervidae*) in North America.

However, now that we know there are no buffalo or antelope in America, it becomes obvious that we should amend an error that has endured for over 140 years and begin singing this iconic song correctly.

(Ok, sing along with me, now)

"Oh, give me a home,
Where the *Bovidae* roam,
And the deer and the *Antilocapridae* play . . . ."

– Lawrence C. Gambone

After all, would you be happy if everyone called your dog a cat? - LCG

Thought for Today (February 24)

THE "DUH?" DEPARTMENT

"Why do they cover Paul's songs but never mine?"

- Yoko Ono

. . . well, duuuh, Yoko? - LCG

Thought for Today (February 25)

THE "POPULAR POLITICAL POLEMICS" DEPARTMENT

"The less people know about how sausages and laws are made, the better they'll sleep at night."

- Otto von Bismarck

. . . maybe there should be a law made about sausages. - LCG

Thought for Today (February 26)

THE "THE TRUTH AND NOTHING BUT" DEPARTMENT

"Men are liars. We'll lie about lying if we have to. I'm an algebra liar. I figure two good lies make a positive."

- Tim Allen

"In real life, I assure you, there is no such thing as algebra."

- Fran Lebowitz

Thought for Today (February 27)

THE "UP IN SMOKE" DEPARTMENT

"Smoking is one of the leading causes of statistics."
– Fletcher Knebel

"It took willpower; but I finally gave up trying to quit smoking." - Chris Cassatt

"To cease smoking is the easiest thing. I ought to know. I've done it a thousand times." - Mark Twain

"Smoking kills. If you're killed, you've lost a very important part of your life." - Brooke Shields

---

CIGARETTE: Tobacco, paper, fire at one end . . . fool at the other. - LCG

Thought for Today (February 28)

THE "DO YOU HAVE A BOARDING PASS?" DEPARTMENT

"There are no passengers on Spaceship Earth. We are all crew." - Marshall McLuhan

---

. . . . some of us are stowaways. - LCG

MARCH

March

Which god gets a planet *and* a month named after him? You guessed it: Mars.

March (Latin: *Martius*) was the original beginning of the year in the 10-month Roman calendar, and the time for the resumption of war. Thus, it was named *Martius* for the god of war.

King Numa Pompilius, added the months of January and February around 713 BCE, so that the calendar covered a standard lunar year (354 days). This led eventually to March's transition to the third month of the year.[11]

March was called *March* or *Marche* in Middle English.

----

[11] January and February were added to the Roman calendar around 713 BCE and became the first and second months of the year around 450 BCE. - LCG

Thought for Today (March 1)

THE "DON'T GET BLOWN AWAY" DEPARTMENT

"The pessimist complains about the wind. The optimist expects it to change. The realist adjusts the sails."
- William A, Ward

. . . the opportunist invests in a wind farm. - LCG

Thought for Today (March 2)

THE "WHY WORRY?" DEPARTMENT

"Remember, today is the tomorrow you worried about yesterday." - Dale Carnegie

----

. . . and we all know yesterday never comes. - LCG

Thought for Today (March 3)

THE "AND CALLED IT MACARONI" DEPARTMENT

"I only know two tunes: one of them is 'Yankee Doodle,' and the other isn't." - Ulysses S. Grant

----

Yeah, and I'll bet it isn't "Twinkle, Twinkle, Little Star" either. - LCG

Thought for Today (March 4)

THE "DATING IS A DRAG" DEPARTMENT

March 4th is the only day that
is both a date and a sentence.

. . . but April May count for something. - LCG

Thought for Today (March 5)

THE "CULINARY QUIPS" DEPARTMENT

"Cabbage: a familiar kitchen-garden vegetable about as
large and wise as a man's head." - Ambrose Bierce

. . . and what does that say for rutabaga? - LCG

Thought for Today (March 6)

THE "CLEAN SWEEP" DEPARTMENT

"My husband has a riding lawnmower; how come there are
no riding vacuum cleaners?" – Terry (Gambone) Rapp

Terry is my sister. And when she made this statement, I responded,
"What's the matter, tired of riding your broom?" She hit me. - LCG

Thought for Today (March 7)

THE "TELL IT LIKE IT IS" DEPARTMENT

"Freedom of speech is important — if you have anything to say. I've checked the internet; nobody does."

- P.J. O'Rourke

. . . . No comment! - LCG

Thought for Today (March 8)

THE "INTERNATIONAL WOMEN'S DAY" DEPARTMENT

"The woman who follows the crowd will usually go no further than the crowd. The woman who walks alone is likely to find herself in places no one has ever been before." - Albert Einstein

----

The first observance of a Women's Day was held on February 28, 1909 in New York; however, March 8 was suggested by the 1910 International Woman's Conference to become an "International Woman's Day." After women gained suffrage in Soviet Russia in 1917, March 8 became a national holiday there, and, until it was adopted in 1975 by the United Nations, the day was celebrated predominantly by the socialist movement and communist countries. - LCG

Thought for Today (March 9)

THE "WORDS OF WISDOM" DEPARTMENT

"Of all the properties which belong to honorable men, not one is so highly prized as that of character."

- Henry Clay (1777-1852)

. . . so, that's why everybody calls me a "character!" - LCG

Thought for Today (March 10)

THE "TELL IT LIKE IT IS" DEPARTMENT

"There's no trick to being a humorist when you have the whole government working for you." - Will Rogers

---

If all the world is a stage, then Congress is the song and dance troupe!
- LCG

Thought for Today (March 11)

THE "NO REGRETS" DEPARTMENT

"Of course I have regrets; but if you are 60 years old and you have no regrets then you haven't lived."

- Christy Moore

. . . it would be regretful if you regret having a life full of regrets. - LCG

Thought for Today (March 12)

THE "CROSS THIS ONE OFF" DEPARTMENT

"I love crossword puzzles. When I die I want to be buried 6 down and 3 across." - Chris Cassatt

---

. . . what's a six-letter word for "coffin?" - LCG

Thought for Today (March 13)

THE "POLITICAL PROSELYTIZATION?" DEPARTMENT

"Too little liberty brings stagnation and too much brings chaos." - Bertrand Russell

---

So, Bertrand . . . what is the right amount? - LCG

Thought for Today (March 14)

THE "IMAGINE THAT" DEPARTMENT

"Anyone who lives within their means suffers from a lack of imagination." - Oscar Wilde (1854-1900)

Anyone who lives within their means has a lot more money than I do.
- LCG

Thought for Today (March 15)

THE "LIKKER IS QUIKKER" DEPARTMENT

"I finally got me a woman who said those six words I wanted to hear: 'My dad owns a liquor store.'"

- Mark Klein

. . . Beer. It's not just for breakfast anymore. - LCG

Thought for Today (March 16)

THE "HISTORICAL TIMELINE" DEPARTMENT

"History and its enigmatic lesson ... nothing changes and yet everything is completely different."

- Aldous Huxley

Aldous Leonard Huxley (26 July 1894 – 22 November 1963) was an English writer and philosopher best known for his novel *Brave New World* published in 1932. - LCG

. . . Chrysostomus?? . . . . Really??

Thought for Today (March 17)

THE "BANANA-RAMA" DEPARTMENT

INTERESTING FACT:

The banana is not a tree, but an herb; the largest known plant without a woody stem or solid trunk.

"Take a piece of the inside of the banana peel and gently rub it around on your teeth for about two minutes. The amazing minerals in the peel like potassium, magnesium and manganese absorb into your teeth and whiten them." - Jorge Valera

Thought for Today (March 18)

THE "ONCE A PUN A TIME" DEPARTMENT

An invisible man married an invisible woman.
Their kids were nothing to look at either.

I wondered why the baseball kept getting bigger.
Then it hit me.

She was only a simple whiskey maker,
but he loved her still.

If we receive a bust of our likeness;
have we gotten a head of ourselves?

Could crop circles be the work of a cereal killer?

If a soldier survives mustard gas and pepper spray,
is he a seasoned veteran?

A girl said she recognized me from the vegetarian club,
but I'd never met herbivore.

I went to a theatrical performance about puns.
It was a play on words.

No matter how much you push the envelope,
it still will be stationery.

What do you get when you toss a hand grenade into a
French kitchen? Linoleum Blownapart.

"A pun is the lowest form of humor—when you don't think of it first."
- Oscar Levant

Thought for Today (March 19)

THE ". . . COUNTDOWN" DEPARTMENT

"The hardest arithmetic to master is that which enables us to count our blessings." - Eric Hoffer

----

. . . because we forget too often that it is our blessings that count. - LCG

Thought for Today (March 20)

THE "WHO NEEDS A MARRIAGE COUNSELOR?" DEPARTMENT

"All marriages are happy. It's the living together afterward that causes all the trouble." - Raymond Hull

----

Marriage means commitment . . . of course, so does insanity. - LCG

Thought for Today (March 21)

THE "LET'S ALL GET ALONG" DEPARTMENT

"My idea of an agreeable person is a person who agrees with me." - Benjamin Disraeli (1804-1881)

. . . I agree with that. - LCG

Thought for Today (March 22)

THE "STATE OF THE ART" DEPARTMENT

"Popular art doesn't last very long. Shakespeare is a different matter. Who does Gilbert and Sullivan now? Yet, 150 years ago, no one was more popular. Already Rodgers and Hammerstein are considered quaint. When I was in my teens and 20s, they were immortals. I wonder if anyone will be doing my musicals in 100 years?"

– Stephen Sondheim

A "Broadway Giant," Stephen Sondheim, born March 22, 1930, became a lyricist and composer during his teen years. Since then, he has won eight Tony Awards, eight Grammy Awards, an Oscar (original song for *Dick Tracy*), and a Pulitzer Prize. At the time of this printing, he is alive still; and collaborating on new musicals. - LCG

Thought for Today (March 23)

THE "HERE, FIDO!" DEPARTMENT

"A dog teaches a boy fidelity, perseverance, and to turn around three times before lying down." - Robert Benchley

----

My dog loves me unconditionally, even though I get angry at her and call her names . . . and I love her unconditionally, even when she does the same. - LCG

Thought for Today (March 24)

THE "INTERESTING FACT" DEPARTMENT

By weight, the sun is 70% hydrogen, 28% helium, 1.5% carbon, nitrogen, and oxygen, and 0.5% all other elements.

"At rest, however, in the middle of everything is the sun."
- Nicolaus Copernicus

Thought for Today (March 25)

THE "WORDS TO PONDER" DEPARTMENT

"Beauty is an outward gift, which is seldom despised, except by those to whom it has been refused."
- Edward Gibbon

On the bright side, aging isn't quite so tragic for those of us who were not born beautiful. - LCG

Thought for Today (March 26)

THE "KEEP IT SIMPLE, STUPID" DEPARTMENT

"If the human brain were so simple that we could understand it, we would be so simple that we couldn't."
- Emerson M. Pugh

. . . it's simple; we're simply not that simple. - LCG

Thought for Today (March 27)

THE "EVERY DAY ECONOMICS" DEPARTMENT

"Inflation is when you pay $15 for the $10 haircut you used to get for $5 when you had hair." - Bob Hope

---

"Inflation is taxation without legislation." - Milton Friedman

Thought for Today (March 28)

THE "HOW TO DO IT" DEPARTMENT

"A formula for success? It's quite simple, really. Double your rate of failure."
- Thomas J. Watson (founder of IBM)

I tripled my failure rate . . . and it worked! I am now a success at failing. - LCG

Thought for Today (March 29)

THE "THE ECONOMICS OF LIFE" DEPARTMENT

I'm a living economy: My hairline's in recession, my waist is going through a period of inflation, my sense of accomplishment is undervalued, and because of it all, I'm in a depression. - L. C. Gambone

---

Bald, fat, stupid, and depressed just about says it all. - LCG

Thought for Today (March 30)

THE "ATTITUDINAL ADJUSTMENT" DEPARTMENT

"A positive attitude may not solve all your problems, but it will annoy enough people to make it worth the effort."
                                                   - Herm Albright

---

This is true . . . I'm positive! - LCG

Thought for Today (March 31)

THE "FUN IS FUN" DEPARTMENT

10 FUN FACTS!

1. You can't wash your eyes with soap.
2. You can't count all the hairs on your head.
3 You can't breathe through your nose with your tongue out.
4. You just tried number 3.
6 When you did number 3, you realized that it is possible ... but you look like a dog.
7. You're smiling right now because you were fooled.
8. You skipped number 5.
9. You just checked to see if there was a number 5.
10. You are not quite sure if this was fun or not (it was).

5. Today is a Great Day!

I can breathe through my mouth with my nose out. - LCG

Lawrence C. Gambone

APRIL

April

April was the second month of the Roman calendar (March was the first) before January and February were added to the year by King Numa Pompilius around 713 BCE. April was rearranged into the fourth slot in approximately 450 BCE, and was assigned 29 days. An extra day was added with the introduction of the Gregorian calendar by Pope Gregory XIV in 1582, which increased the days to 30.

No one is sure how April got its name; however, there are a few common theories. One is that the name is rooted in the Latin name *Aprilis*, which is derived from the Latin *aperire* meaning "to open" — which could be a reference to the opening or blossoming of flowers and trees, a common occurrence throughout the month of April in the northern hemisphere.

Another theory holds that since months are often named for gods and goddess, and since *Aphrilis* is derived from the Greek "Aphrodite," April, the theory proposes, was named for the Greek goddess of love (the goddess that the Romans called "Venus").

A third theory that adds to the confusion proposes that April is named after the goddess *Eostre*.[12] Around the 5th century CE, the Anglo-Saxons referred to April as *Eostre-monath*, (*monath* meaning "month") a reference to *Eostre*, whose feast was celebrated during the month.

---

[12] *Eostre* is the Germanic Goddess of Spring. Also called *Ostara* or *Eastre*, She gave her name to the Christian festival of Easter (which is an older Pagan festival appropriated by the Catholic Church), whose timing still is dictated by the Moon.

Thought for Today (April 1)

THE "ALL THE FOOLS ALL THE TIME" DEPARTMENT

"This is the day upon which we are reminded of what we are on the other three hundred and sixty-four."
                                            - Mark Twain

"We're fools whether we dance or not, so we might as well dance." - Japanese Proverb

"The trouble with practical jokes is that very often they get elected." - Will Rogers

"I have great faith in fools—self-confidence, my friends call it." - Edgar Allan Poe

On the first day of April, we should believe nothing and trust no one . . . just like all the other days.
                                            - L. C. Gambone

"A common mistake that people make when trying to design something completely foolproof is to underestimate the ingenuity of complete fools."
                                            - Douglas Adams

I believe April 15 should be "April Fool's Day," because after all, that's the day when everyone tries to fool Uncle Sam. - LCG

Thought for Today (April 2)

THE "WORDS OF WISDUMB" DEPARTMENT

"Fortunately I've been just smart enough to realize that I'm stupid." - Larry Wall

---

Well . . . I'm just stupid enough to think I'm smart. - LCG

Thought for Today (April 3)

THE "PROPHETIC PRONOUNCEMENTS" DEPARTMENT

"Wisdom doesn't necessarily come with age. Sometimes age just shows up all by itself." - Tom Wilson

---

My wife tells me that every day—every day . . . yep, every day! - LCG

Thought for Today (April 4)

THE "ASTROLOGICAL PRONOUNCEMENTS" DEPARTMENT

"I don't believe in astrology; I'm a Sagittarius and we're skeptical." - Arthur C. Clarke

---

I don't believe in psychology; I'm a schizophrenic and we're nuts! - LCG

Thought for Today (April 5)

THE "DO YOU KNOW WHERE YOU ARE?" DEPARTMENT

"I love California. I practically grew up in Phoenix."
- Dan Quayle.

"I have campaigned in all 57 states." - Barack Obama

Honestly, I cannot comment on this. - LCG

Thought for Today (April 6)

THE "TO ERR IS HUMAN" DEPARTMENT

I've made lots of mistakes in my lifetime: SOME were regrettable; MANY could have been avoided; MOST were stupid; ALL were honest." – Lawrence C. Gambone.

It's the "stupid" part that upsets me most. - LCG

Thought for Today (April 7)

THE "PERTINENT PARADIGM" DEPARTMENT

LOGIC: A systematic method employed to achieve the wrong conclusion with confidence.

Sounds logical to me. - LCG

Thought for Today (April 8)

THE "WORDS TO LIVE BY" DEPARTMENT

"Success is not the key to happiness. Happiness is the key to success . . . love what you are doing."

- Herman Cain

Forget success; I'd be happy if I could find my keys. - LCG

Thought for Today (April 9)

THE "LEARN IT FROM THE LEHRER" DEPARTMENT

"If, after hearing my songs, just one human being is inspired to say something nasty to a friend or, perhaps to strike a loved one, it will all have been worth the while."

– Tom Lehrer

Alive still at the time of this printing, Thomas Andrew Lehrer (born April 9, 1928) is a retired singer-songwriter, satirist, and mathematician. He has lectured on mathematics and musical theater. He is best known for the pithy, humorous songs he recorded in the 1950s and 1960s.

"Lehrer" means "teacher" in German. - LCG

Thought for Today (April 10)

THE "SIGNIFICANT EVENTS" DEPARTMENT

THE FOLLOWING EVENTS TOOK PLACE APRIL 10:[13]

1849 - Inventor Walter Hunt patented the safety pin in New York City; selling the rights for $400.

1970 - Paul McCartney announced the official split of *The Beatles*.

I wonder if McCartney could have used Hunt's safety pin to hold the group together? - LCG

Thought for Today (April 11)

THE "SOMETHING TO THINK ABOUT" DEPARTMENT

"Striving for success without hard work is like trying to harvest where you haven't planted." - David Bly

---

Hard work is hard (yep, you read it here first, folks). - LCG

---

[13] https://www.onthisday.com/events/april/10 (accessed 6/17/18)

Thought for Today (April 12)

THE "DAFFYNITIONS" DEPARTMENT

Several years ago, the *Washington Post's* Style invitational asked readers to take any word, change one or more of its letters, and supply a new definition. Here are some winners:

BOZONE LAYER: The substance surrounding stupid people that stops bright ideas from penetrating.

COKECAN ADDICTION: The uncontrollable urge to buy cases and cases of soda.

DECAFALON: The grueling event of getting through the day without the added help of caffeine.

FEES: What a photographer tells a group of lawyers to say to make them smile.

HIPATITAS: Terminal coolness.

HYPENOTIZE: Becoming mesmerized into believing the product claims made by advertisers are true.

OSTEOPORNOSIS: A degenerate disease.

PSYCHO PATH: The route the deranged take when traveling through a forest.

SARCHASM: The gulf between the author of sarcastic wit and the person who doesn't get it.

VIOLINENCE: Occurs when a person plays a "mean violin."

Thought for Today (April 13)

THE "NOTEWORTHY BIRTHDAY" DEPARTMENT

Thomas Jefferson

Thomas Jefferson was an American Founding Father who was principal author of the Declaration of Independence.[14] Jefferson was elected the second Vice President[15] of the United States, serving under John Adams. He was elected third President of the United States in 1800.

Born: April 13, 1743, Shadwell, VA
Died: July 4, 1826, Charlottesville, VA
Preceded by: John Adams
Succeeded by: James Madison
Children: Martha Jefferson Randolph, Eston Hemings

Quotes

- *The tree of liberty must be refreshed from time to time with the blood of patriots and tyrants.*
- *In matters of style, swim with the current; in matters of principle, stand like a rock.*
- *I hold it, that a little rebellion, now and then, is a good thing, and as necessary in the political world as storms in the physical.*

---

[14] https://en.wikipedia.org/wiki/Thomas_Jefferson (accessed 6/17/18)

[15] . . . at that time the Vice President was elected separately from the President.

Thought for Today (April 14)

THE "UPCOMING TAX DAY" DEPARTMENT

We all know that politicians do no work and receive payments from the government.

. . . Technically, isn't that the definition of welfare?

- L. C. Gambone

. . . it is obvious to me that politicians fare well. - LCG

Thought for Today (April 15)

THE "TAX DAY OF INFAMY" DEPARTMENT

WE'VE GOT WHAT IT TAKES
TO TAKE WHAT YOU'VE GOT!

Internal Revenue Service Motto

"Taxation with representation ain't so hot either." - Gerald Barzan

"There may be liberty and justice for all, but there are tax breaks only for some." - Martin A. Sullivan

"It's every American's duty to support his government, but not necessarily in the style to which it has become accustomed."
- Thomas Clifford

Thought for Today (April 16)

THE "BETTER LEFT UNSAID" DEPARTMENT

"Gossip is the art of saying nothing in a way that leaves nothing unsaid." - Walter Winchell

---

So, you say something that means nothing; and, you say nothing that means something . . . is this a case of something for nothing? - LCG

Thought for Today (April 17)

THE "BILLION-DOLLAR LOTTERY" DEPARTMENT

"All I ask is the chance to prove that money can't make me happy." - Spike Milligan

"I've done the calculation and your chances of winning the lottery are identical whether you play or not."
– Fran Lebowitz

"Here's something to think about: How come you never see a headline like 'Psychic Wins Lottery'?" – Jay Leno

---

"Win not, you will." - Yoda

Thought for Today (April 18)

THE "MAY THE FARCE BE WITH YOU" DEPARTMENT

The JEDI ACADEMY
JEDI TEMPLE, Coruscant

DATE: Long ago . . .

STUDENT REPORT CARD - Yoda

Course Name	Course Number	Grade
Light Saber	401	A+
Philosophy	301	A
Applied Force	404	A+
Quantum Mechanics	201	A
Physics	301	A
Calculus	301	A
English Grammar	101	F

"Care not, do I, for report cards." - Yoda

Thought for Today (April 19)

THE "STUFF YOU NEVER THOUGHT ABOUT" DEPARTMENT

Why is Wednesday spelled . . . well, ah, Wednesday?

The name Wednesday is derived from the Old English *Wōdnesdæg* meaning, "day of Woden" (or Odin, as he is known today). Woden was an Anglo-Saxon god associated with healing, death, royalty, the gallows, knowledge, battle, sorcery, poetic inspiration, curing horses, the runic alphabet, and carrying off the dead (I mean, really, did this guy have a "full plate," or what?).

So, Wednesday comes from *Wōdnesdæg*, or Woden's day, which became transposed somehow in Middle English to *Weodnesdei*. However, getting to *Weodnesdei* wasn't easy, since Middle English rules governing spelling were lax to say the least. As a result, Woden's day has gone through various transformations: It has been seen in letters and manuscripts as *wodnesdaeg*, *Wenysday*, *wonysday*, *Weddinsday*, and finally, *Weodnesdei*.

Shakespeare tried to match pronunciation by spelling the day (very reasonably, in my opinion), "Wensday." However, it didn't stick. In Modern English, Woden got to keep his "d" and his day; and currently, it is spelled, "Wednesday."

. . . personally, I like "wonysday." - LCG

Thought for Today (April 20)

THE "FEMININE FASHION FORMAT" DEPARTMENT

"Women dress alike all over the world: they dress to be annoying to other women." - Elsa Schiaparelli

---

"Men like cars, women like clothes. Women only like cars because they take them to clothes." - Rita Rudner

Thought for Today (April 21)

THE "HELPFUL THOUGHTS" DEPARTMENT

"Why pay a dollar for a bookmark? Why not use the dollar for a bookmark?" - Steven Spielberg

---

It doesn't matter, Steve, nobody reads books anymore . . . and nobody has a dollar. - LCG

Thought for Today (April 22)

THE "HAIKU TO YOU, TOO" DEPARTMENT

AUTHOR'S NOTE: First observed in 1970, "Earth Day" is celebrated each year on April 22.

A few years ago, for Earth Day, one of the nature websites held a nature poetry contest. I submitted the following poem, which I thought to be rather original. The judges thought otherwise. It didn't win; in fact, they refused even to acknowledge it. - LCG

Gravity
A poetic travesty
It rhymes with two words only
One is "cavity"
The other word is "depravity"
So, it's hard to write a poem about
Gravity

. . . Honestly, I didn't think it was so bad. - LCG

Thought for Today (April 23)

THE "TO BE, OR NOT TO BE" DEPARTMENT

William Shakespeare (1564-1616)[16] is considered to be the ultimate Elizabethan playwright.

Shakespeare was born April 23, 1564 (St. George's Day) and died on his birthday, April 23, 1616, age 52.

In 1582, Shakespeare applied to marry Anne Whateley, apparently a scribe error, because he married Anne Hathaway in 1582 and had 3 children: Susanna (1583), Judith and Hamnet (twins 1585).

William Shakespeare was only 18 years old when he married Anne Hathaway, who was 26 years old at the time.

Shakespeare began writing in 1592. There is a gap in the evidence . . . no one knows what he did between 1585 and 1592.

There is so much more information about Billy Shakespeare; much more than I have room for here . . . tomes have been written about him; and, of course, he wrote tomes himself. - LCG

---

[16] https://en.wikipedia.org/wiki/William_Shakespeare (accessed 6/17/18)

Thought for Today (April 24)

THE "YOU READ IT ON THE ROAD" DEPARTMENT

BUMPER STICKER:

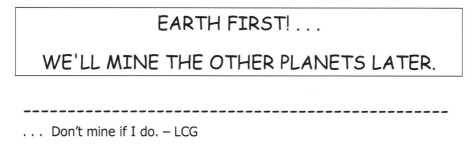

EARTH FIRST! . . .

WE'LL MINE THE OTHER PLANETS LATER.

. . . Don't mine if I do. – LCG

Thought for Today (April 25)

THE "GIVE ATTITUDE SOME LATITUDE!" DEPARTMENT

"A happy person is not a person in a certain set of circumstances, but with a certain set of attitudes."

- Hugh Downs

"A negative attitude yields negative results; a positive attitude yields negative results." – Heave Up (website)

My negative attitude is much more positive than yours. - LCG

Thought for Today (April 26)

THE "RINGS AND RADIATION" DEPARTMENT

On April 26, 1514, Astronomer and Mathematician, Nicolaus Copernicus, made his first observations of the planet Saturn.

Also . . . On April 26, 1986, the world's worst nuclear accident occurred at the Chernobyl power plant in the Soviet Union.

An explosion and fire occurred in the Number 4 reactor sending radioactivity into the atmosphere; killing at least 31 people immediately, and creating a residual radiation problem that has made the once vibrant city uninhabitable. However, Chernobyl will recover—experts have determined that the city will become habitable again in approximately 20,000 years.

A mere 472 years separate the discovery of one planet and the trashing of another. - LCG

Thought for Today (April 27)

THE "COMPUTER MESSAGES WE'D LIKE TO SEE" DEPARTMENT

Sado-Masochistic Computer: Hit Any Key!

Windows Alert!

Windows has not had an error in the past 10 minutes!

There's no real message.
We're just proud of ourselves right now.

. . . Must be some kinda glitch! – LCG

Thought for Today (April 28)

THE "WORDS OF WISDUMB" DEPARTMENT

"Good Judgment" Comes From Experience
. . . Which Comes From "Bad Judgment."

. . . and judging from this quote, I have lots of "Experience." - LCG

Thought for Today (April 29)

THE "POLITICAL PROSELYTIZATION" DEPARTMENT

What is the difference between despotism and democracy?

Actually, the only difference is perception. In the former, the elite few appoint the corrupt several to rule the incompetent many. In the latter, the elite few allow the incompetent many to believe incorrectly that they elect the elite few who appoint the corrupt several to rule the incompetent many.

Therefore, I have coined a new word, which I believe better describes our mislabeled political system:

Instead of "democracy," I submit, respectfully, that our political system should be termed **"Despomockeracy;"** which is defined as the **Despotic Mockery** of what we believe foolishly to be true **Democracy**. – LCG

"Despomockeracy" . . . it makes sense to me. - LCG

Thought for Today (April 30)

THE "IN WITH THE GOOD, OUT WITH THE BAD" DEPARTMENT[17]

On April 30, 1789, George Washington was inaugurated as the first President of the United States of America.

On April 30, 1945, Adolf Hitler, along with Eva Braun, his wife of one day, committed suicide in the Fuhrerbunker in Berlin as Red Army troops captured the city.

. . . good and bad all on the same day (albeit 156 years apart). - LCG

---

[17] https://www.onthisday.com/events/april/30 (accessed 6/17/18)

Lawrence C. Gambone

MAY

May

May (Latin *Maius*) is the fifth month of the year in the Julian and Gregorian Calendars. Common convention holds that May was named for either the Greek or Roman goddess, both of whom were named *Maia*. In Roman literature, *Maia* was identified with the goddess of fertility, *Bona Dea*, whose festival was held in May.

However, the Roman poet Ovid provides a second etymology, in which he says that the month of May is named for the *maiores*, Latin for "elders," and that the following month (June) is named for the *iuniores*, or "young people"

Thought for Today (May 1)

THE "HOLLYWOOD HISTORY" DEPARTMENT

"Citizen Kane," directed by Orson Welles and starring himself, Joseph Cotton, and Dorothy Corningore, premiered at the Palace Theater in New York City on May 1, 1941.[18]

Citizen Kane has been called the greatest film ever made. In 1989, the United States Library of Congress deemed the film "culturally, historically, or aesthetically significant" and selected it for preservation in the National Film Registry; one of the first 25 films inducted into the registry. In 2012, the Motion Picture Editors Guild published a list of the 75 best-edited films of all time based on a survey of its membership. Citizen Kane was listed second.

The film currently has a 100% rating at *Rotten Tomatoes*, based on 75 reviews by approved critics, with an average rating of 9.4 out of 10. The site's consensus states: "Orson Welles's epic tale of a publishing tycoon's rise and fall is entertaining, poignant, and inventive in its storytelling, earning its reputation as a landmark achievement in film."

Nevertheless, there is some controversy. Ingmar Bergman disliked the film and called it ". . . a total bore." Personally, I agree. It was boring. My Opinion: A movie is not art necessarily, just because it was filmed in black and white. - LCG

---

[18] https://en.wikipedia.org/wiki/Citizen_Kane (accessed 6/17/18)

Thought for Today (May 2)

THE "WORDS TO PONDER/THINK ABOUT" DEPARTMENT

"Think like a man of action, act like a man of thought."
— Henri Louis Bergson

I'll take action on this thought . . . I think. - LCG

Thought for Today (May 3)

THE "CLASSICAL WISDOM" DEPARTMENT

"We hang the petty thieves and appoint the great ones to public office." - Aesop (620-560 BCE)

True yesterday; true today — proof positive that, when the subject is politics, nothing has changed. - LCG

Thought for Today (May 4)

THE "LESSONS IN LIFE" DEPARTMENT

The first step to getting the things you want out of life is this: Decide what you want.

Make peace with your past so it doesn't screw up the present.

It isn't enough to be forgiven by others. You have to learn to forgive yourself.

If you can't control your attitude, rest assured that it will control you.

Sometimes you have the right to be angry; you never have the right to be cruel.

We're living in exponential times. It is not business as usual.

You may live only once; but if you work it right, once is enough.

Remember: The main thing is to keep the main thing the main thing.
- LCG

Thought for Today (May 5)

THE "MEXICAN HISTORY" DEPARTMENT

CINCO DE MAYO

AUTHOR'S NOTE: Cinco De Mayo commemorates the battle of Puebla which lasted from daybreak to early evening on May 5, 1862. Often, people outside of Mexico confuse Cinco De Mayo with Mexican Independence, which was declared 41 years earlier on September 28, 1821.[19]

In the battle, General Ignacio Zaragoza, who was born in Texas, defended Puebla with a rag-tag band of 2,000 Mexicans against a superior force of 6,000 French Soldiers. The French retreated finally, having lost over 500 soldiers. The Mexicans lost less than 100 men.

Although not a major strategic win in the overall war against the French, Zaragoza's success at Puebla bolstered the resistance movement.[20]

Four years after the battle, in November 1866, thanks in part to US military and political support, France withdrew its last troops unceremoniously from Mexico.

----

[19] However, Mexican Independence is celebrated on September 16. On that date in 1810, in the town of Dolores, Miguel Hidalgo, a leader of the independence movement, motivated people to revolt against the Spanish regime with his cry for independence, "El Grito de la Independencia!"

[20] So, let me get this straight: Cinco de Mayo celebrates a battle (not Mexican Independence); the battle did not result in a true Mexican victory; its hero was born in Texas; and Mexican independence is celebrated September 16 even though its actual date is September 28. Wow! Where's the tequila? - LCG

Thought for Today (May 6)

THE "TELL IT LIKE IT IS" DEPARTMENT

"Oh, you hate your job? Why didn't you say so? There's a support group for that. It's called EVERYBODY, and they meet at the bar." – Drew Carey

----

. . . Now, there's a meeting I don't mind attending. - LCG

Thought for Today (May 7)

THE "HOW DO YOU ACCOUNT FOR THIS?" DEPARTMENT

Twenty-four hours in a day

Twenty-four beers in a case

. . . Coincidence?

. . . I think not! - LCG

Thought for Today (May 8)

THE "ON THIS DAY IN HISTORY" DEPARTMENT

EVENTS OF INTEREST THAT OCCURRED ON MAY 8:[21]

1521 - The parliament of Worms installed an edict against Martin Luther.

1541 - Spanish explorer Hernando de Soto discovered the Mississippi River.

1831 - The first installment of Hans Christian Andersen's "Fairy Tales" was published in Copenhagen, Denmark.

1933 - Mohandas Gandhi began a 21-day fast in protest against British oppression in India.

1945 - German General Wilhelm Keitel surrendered formally to Marshal Georgy Zhukov and the Soviets in Berlin.

. . . and there you have it! - LCG

---

[21] https://www.onthisday.com/events/may/8 (accessed 6/17/18)

Thought for Today (May 9)

THE "GIMME A BREAK" DEPARTMENT

"It's never crowded along the extra mile." - Wayne Dyer

... could that be because the road was closed? - LCG

Thought for Today (May 10)

THE "MOTHER'S DAY" DEPARTMENT

"Don't forget Mother's Day, or as they call it in Beverly Hills, Dad's Third Wife's Day." - Jay Leno

---

"Mother's Day" is an American holiday held traditionally on the second Sunday in May. - LCG

Thought for Today (May 11)

THE "AGRICULTURE AGGRANDIZEMENT" DEPARTMENT

. . . AND THAT AIN'T NO CORN

Set in medieval England, a recent movie had a scene in which a landowner and his servant talked about planting corn. I found this interesting, since it is well known that corn is indigenous to the western hemisphere or "new world," and did not reach Europe (from America) until the early 16th century. Even then, it took nearly a century to become cultivated widely in the "old world," where now it is a staple crop. Thus, the film appeared anachronous: Early 13th century British farmers did not plant corn.

So, unsurprisingly, did Hollywood get it wrong once again? Well, in this case, perhaps not. The word "corn" has many different meanings depending on what country you are in:[22] Corn is called maize or Indian corn in the United States. In some countries, corn means the leading crop grown in a certain district: Corn in England means wheat; in Scotland and Ireland, it refers to oats. Most likely, corn mentioned in the Bible refers to wheat or barley.

---

[22] https://en.wikipedia.org/wiki/Maize (accessed 6/17/18)

"Corn" as we know it today, evolved in the western hemisphere. Evidence of corn's early presence was identified from pollen grains, considered to be 80,000 years old, obtained from drill cores 200 feet below Mexico City.

TRIVIA QUESTION: Is Corn A Vegetable Or Fruit?

Well, actually . . . .

The DNA profile of modern corn dates back 9,000 years to a teosinte grass from the tropical Central Balsas River Valley of southern Mexico. This makes southern Mexico the "cradle" of maize evolution. Excavations of caves and shelters in this region unearthed stone milling tools that contained maize residues. The oldest tools were found in a layer of deposits that is 8,700 years old. They remain the oldest physical evidence of maize use to date.

At first glance, teosinte would seem to be a very unlikely parent. It has skinny ears, with a dozen kernels wrapped inside stone-hard casings, that do not resemble in any way today's modern corn cobs with their many rows of naked kernels. In fact, teosinte was classified at first as a closer relative to rice than to maize.

But the DNA evidence is succinct; teosinte is the parent plant of corn. What is amazing is the fact that humans 9,000 years ago were able to transform a grass with many inconvenient, unwanted features into a high-yielding, easily harvested food crop. Most likely, this took hundreds, or even thousands, of years to accomplish.

But the result is impressive indeed. Corn, as we know it today, is a human invention. The plant does not exist in the wild. It would not—could not—exist except by human cultivation and protection. – Lawrence C. Gambone

---

HINT: Now you have another phenomenal trivia question. Ask your friends if corn is a vegetable or a fruit. After they guess incorrectly (and, most likely, they will), impress them by disclosing that it is grass. For proof, tell them to buy this book. - LCG

Thought for Today (May 12)

THE "HAPPY BIRTHDAY" DEPARTMENT

Yogi Berra

New York Yankees legend Lorenzo Pietro "Yogi" Berra was born May 12, 1924, and died at age 90 on September 22, 2015.[23] Berra was an 18-time Major League All-Star, appearing in 14 World Series—winning 10 of them—as a member of the Yankees.

Berra's contributions to Major League Baseball (MLB) history are incalculable. He is considered to be one of the greatest catchers in major league history (he caught the only post season "perfect game" in major league history), coached for several years, and he was inducted into the MLB hall of fame.

---

[23] https://en.wikipedia.org/wiki/Yogi_Berra (accessed 6/17/18)

But Yogi's legacy is better remembered for the malapropisms (called Berra-isms) that he contributed to the American language. Sports writers and newscasters were thrilled to interview Yogi, since they could count on him always to come up with a "gem."

Berra-isms have been defined as "colloquial expressions that lack logic;" and they are countless. In fact, many are attributed to Berra even though, in actuality, he may never have said them. His apt response to this: "I never said most of the things I said."

Here are some of my favorite Berra-isms:

- You can observe a lot by just watching.
- It ain't over till it's over.
- It's just like déjà vu all over again.
- No one goes there nowadays, it's too crowded.
- Baseball is 90% mental and the other half is physical.
- A nickel ain't worth a dime anymore.
- Always go to other people's funerals, otherwise they won't come to yours.
- You wouldn't have won if we'd beaten you.
- Slump? I ain't in no slump...I just ain't hitting.
- The future ain't what it used to be.
- It gets late early out here.
- If the people don't want to come out to the ballpark, nobody's going to stop them.
- Pair up in threes.

- You've got to be very careful if you don't know where you are going, because you might not get there.
- He hits from both sides of the plate. He's amphibious.
- It was impossible to get a conversation going, everybody was talking too much.
- Take it with a grin of salt.
- The towels were so thick there I could hardly close my suitcase.
- Little League baseball is a very good thing because it keeps the parents off the streets.

Yogi Berra died on September 22, which is my birthday, which is a fact that has no relevance whatsoever to this "Thought for Today." - LCG

Thought for Today (May 13)

THE "COSMIC COMMENTS" DEPARTMENT

"I may not have gone where I intended to go, but I think I have ended up where I needed to be." – Douglas Adams

---

. . . I need to be in a bar! - LCG

Thought for Today (May 14)

THE "POLITICAL PRONOUNCEMENTS" DEPARTMENT

"There ought to be one day—just one—when there is open season on senators." - Will Rogers

---

I vote "Yes;" but . . . senators only? - LCG

Thought for Today (May 15)

THE "OPINIONS COUNT" DEPARTMENT

"Man is rated the highest animal, at least among all animals who returned the questionnaire." - Robert Brault

---

A questionnaire to determine the obvious—who Brault that up? - LCG

Thought for Today (May 16)

THE "SCIENTIFIC PONTIFICATION" DEPARTMENT

"If we knew what we were doing, it wouldn't be called research, would it?" - Albert Einstein

---

. . . Yeah, I keep losing stuff and have to re-search for it over and over again! - LCG

Thought for Today (May 17)

THE "SONGS WE'D LIKE TO HEAR" DEPARTMENT

"Mack the Knife" - Julius Caesar

"Cats" - Dog the Bounty Hunter

"America The Beautiful" - Osama Bin Laden

"Roll Over Beethoven" - Wolfgang Amadeus Mozart

"Stand By Your Man" - Hillary Clinton

"I Did It My Way" - Milli Vanilli

"Hold That Tiger" - Siegfried and Roy

"I've Got Plenty of Nothing" - Bill Gates

Unlike Bill, I started out with plenty of nothing . . . and I still have most of it. - LCG

Thought for Today (May 18)

THE "WORDS FROM THE WISE" DEPARTMENT

"If 'A' equals success, then the formula is: A = X + Y + Z. 'X' is work. 'Y' is play. 'Z' is keep your mouth shut."
- Albert Einstein

. . . it's genius, I tell you . . . pure genius. - LCG

Thought for Today (May 19)

THE "LESSONS IN LIFE" DEPARTMENT

LIFE LESSON 101: Never criticize someone until you've walked a mile in their shoes.

. . . then, when you criticize them, you'll be a mile away . . . and you'll have their shoes! - LCG

Thought for Today (May 20)

THE "HELPFUL HOME HINTS" DEPARTMENT

"If you don't want your dog to have bad breath, do what I do: Pour some Lavoris in the toilet." - Jay Leno

---

. . . my dog never drinks from the toilet . . . she's too short! - LCG

Thought for Today (May 21)

THE "WRIGHT IS NEVER WRONG" DEPARTMENT

"I almost had a psychic girlfriend, but she left me before we met." - Steven Wright

---

I almost had a girlfriend, but she refused to meet me. - LCG

Thought for Today (May 22)

THE "OBVIOUSLY STATING THE OBVIOUS" DEPARTMENT

"Looking around at what's taking place in politics today, it is easy to get disheartened. Our political discourse—both the kind we see on TV and the kind we experience among each other—did not use to be this bad and it does not have to be this way . . . . when people distrust politics, they come to distrust institutions. They lose faith in their government, and the future too. We can acknowledge this. But we don't have to accept it. And we cannot enable it either."

- Paul Ryan, Speaker of the House

What? There is a possibility that people may distrust politicians and lose faith in their government? And as a politician, is he including himself in this scurrilous diatribe? - LCG

Thought for Today (May 23)

THE "THIS DAY IN HISTORY" DEPARTMENT

EVENTS OF INTEREST THAT OCCURRED MAY 23:[24]

1430 Burgundians capture Joan of Arc and sell her to the English.

1533 Henry VIII's marriage to Catherine of Aragon is declared null and void.

1618 The Thirty Years War begins.

1701 Captain William Kidd, the Scottish pirate, is hanged on the banks of the Thames.

1785 Benjamin Franklin announces his invention of bifocals.

1788 South Carolina, the 8th state, entered the union; its capital is Columbia, and its motto is "Dum Sipro Spero (While I breathe, I hope)."

1861 Pro-Union and pro-Confederate forces clash in western Virginia.

1900 Civil War hero Sgt. William H. Carney becomes the first African American to receive the Medal of Honor, thirty-seven years after the battle of Fort Wagner.

---

[24] https://www.onthisday.com/events/may/23 (last accessed 6/17/18)

1934 Gangsters Bonnie Parker and Clyde Barrow are killed by Texas Rangers.

1945 Heinrich Himmler, head of the Nazi Gestapo, commits suicide after being captured by Allied forces.

1949 The Federal Republic of West Germany is proclaimed.

1960 Israel announces the capture of Nazi Adolf Eichmann in Argentina.

History teaches us . . . well . . . history. - LCG

Thought for Today (May 24)

THE "NO NEWSWORTHY NEWS" DEPARTMENT

Murder, theft, fire, accidents, war, sex, politicians lying and cheating . . . there's never anything new in news.

- L. C. Gambone

. . . Never confuse the news with the truth. - LCG

Thought for Today (May 25)

THE "MEANING OF SUCCESS" DEPARTMENT

"To laugh often and much; to win the respect of intelligent people and the affection of children; to earn the appreciation of honest critics and endure the betrayal of false friends; to appreciate beauty, to find the best in theirs; to leave the world a little better; whether by a healthy child, a garden patch or a redeemed social condition; to know even one life has breathed easier because you have lived. This is the meaning of success."

- Ralph Waldo Emerson

Ralph Waldo Emerson (May 25, 1803 - April 27, 1882) was an American essayist, lecturer, philosopher, and poet. Emerson led the transcendentalist movement of the mid-19th century. He was seen as a champion of individualism and a critic of the countervailing pressures of society. Emerson disseminated his thoughts through dozens of published essays and more than 1,500 public lectures across the United States. - LCG

Thought for Today (May 26)

THE "ENGLISH IS A SECOND LANGUAGE FOR US ALL" DEPARTMENT

PARAPROSDOKIANS:

Yep, believe it or not, "paraprosdokian" is a real word.[25] A paraprosdokian is defined as: "A figure of speech in which the latter part of a sentence or phrase is surprising or unexpected; frequently used in a humorous situation."

To use the more familiar, colloquial expression, a paraprosdokian is a "punch line." The mere fact that a word such as paraprosdokian exists explains why I consider English indeed to be "a second language for us all."

What follows are examples of paraprosdokians:

- Where there's a will, I want to be in it.
- Hurting you may be the last thing I want to do; but it is still on my list.
- Light travels faster than sound, which is why some people appear bright until they speak.
- I'd love to agree with you; but then we'd both be wrong.
- Youth may fade with age; but immaturity can last forever.
- We never really grow up; we just learn how to act in public.

---

[25] https://en.wikipedia.org/wiki/Paraprosdokian (accessed 6/17/18)

- Knowledge is knowing a tomato is a fruit. Wisdom is not putting a tomato in fruit salad.
- Busses stop at a bus station and trains stop at a train station. My desk is a work station.
- I asked God for a bike; but God doesn't work that way. So, I stole a bike and asked God for forgiveness.
- You don't have to outrun a bear . . . you just have to outrun your buddy.
- Change is inevitable; except from a vending machine.
- When you are tempted to fight fire with fire, remember that the fire department uses water.
- I came, I saw, I was bored to death.

Stop worrying about the world ending today. It's already tomorrow in Australia.
– Charles M. Schulz -

If I said that, after reading this, now you have learned something; by definition, that would be a paraprosdokian. - LCG

Thought for Today (May 27)

THE "MODEST AND HUMBLE" DEPARTMENT

"My opinions may have changed, but not the fact that I am right." - Ashleigh Brilliant

---

. . . and my opinion? That's just brilliant, Brilliant. - LCG

Thought for Today (May 28)

THE "VICE VERSA" DEPARTMENT

"To be is to do." - Descartes

"To do is to be." - Voltaire

"Do be do be do." - Sinatra

Do da do da . . . duh? - Gambone

Thought for Today (May 29)

THE "INTERESTING FACTS" DEPARTMENT

EVENTS OF INTEREST THAT OCCURRED MAY 29:[26]

1453 - Constantinople, capital of the Eastern Roman (Byzantine) Empire falls to the Turks under Muhammad II; this ends the Byzantine Empire.

1790 – Rhode Island, the 13th state, entered the Union May 29, 1790. Its capital is Providence, and its motto is, "Hope."

1848 – Wisconsin, the 30th state, entered the Union May 29, 1848. Its capital is Madison, and its motto is, "Forward."

1917 – Born May 29, 1917, John Fitzgerald Kennedy was the first Roman Catholic President. Also, he was the first President born in the 20th century.

2004 - The World War II Memorial was dedicated in Washington, D.C.

----

[26] https://www.onthisday.com/events/may/29 (accessed 6/17/18)

Thought for Today (May 30)

THE "TRIBUTE TO OUR FALLEN HEROES" DEPARTMENT

AUTHOR'S NOTE: Since Memorial Day falls on the last Monday in May, it is hard to pin the holiday to a specific date. Therefore, I selected arbitrarily May 30. - LCG

Decorating soldiers' graves with flowers is an ancient custom that dates back to prehistory.[27] In the United States, soldiers' graves were decorated during the American Civil War. The question becomes, "When and where was the first Memorial Day ceremony?"

In 1906, a claim was made that a Civil War soldier's grave was decorated in Warrenton, Virginia, on June 3, 1861, implying the first Memorial Day occurred there.

Though not for Union soldiers, women in Savannah, Georgia, decorated Confederate soldiers' graves in 1862. The cemetery dedication at Gettysburg, Pennsylvania, in 1863, could be considered a Memorial Day-type of commemoration.

The first widely publicized Memorial Day-type observance after the Civil War occurred on May 1, 1865, in Charleston, South Carolina. There, during the war, Union prisoners of war were held at the Hampton Park Race Course in Charleston; 257 prisoners died there and were buried hastily in unmarked graves. It was the black freedmen of Charleston who cleaned up and landscaped the burial ground, building an enclosure and an arch

[27] https://en.wikipedia.org/wiki/Memorial_Day (accessed 6/17/18)

labeled, "Martyrs of the Race Course." Nearly 10,000 people, mostly freedmen, gathered on May 1 to commemorate the war dead.

A tribute to the Civil War dead occurred in Columbus, Mississippi, April 25, 1866, when a group of women visited a cemetery to decorate the graves of Confederate soldiers who had fallen in battle at Shiloh. Nearby were the graves of Union soldiers, neglected because they were the enemy. Disturbed at the sight of the bare graves, the women placed some of their flowers on those graves as well.

On May 5, 1868, the head of the Grand Army of the Republic, an organization of Union veterans, announced that a "Decoration Day" be established for the nation to decorate the graves of the war dead with flowers.

All in all, approximately 25 places have been named in connection with the origin of Memorial Day, many of them in the South where most of the war dead were buried. By the end of the 19th century, Decoration Day ceremonies were being held on May 30 throughout the nation. State legislatures passed proclamations designating the day; and the Army and Navy adopted regulations for proper observance at their facilities.

It was not until after World War I, however, that the day was expanded to honor those who died in all American wars. In 1966, Congress and President Lyndon Johnson declared Waterloo, New York, the "birthplace" of Decoration (Memorial) Day. There, a ceremony on May 5, 1866, honored local veterans who had fought in the Civil

War. Businesses closed and residents flew flags at half-staff.

In 1971, by an act of Congress, "Decoration Day" was renamed "Memorial Day," declared a national holiday, and designated as the last Monday in May.

NOTE: Many Southern states have established days for honoring Confederate dead. Mississippi celebrates Confederate Memorial Day on the last Monday of April, Alabama on the fourth Monday of April, and Georgia on April 26. North and South Carolina observe it on May 10, Louisiana on June 3, and Tennessee calls that date Confederate Decoration Day. Texas celebrates Confederate Heroes Day January 19, and Virginia calls the last Monday in May Confederate Memorial Day.
- LCG

Thought for Today (May 31)

THE "HIT THE DIRT" DEPARTMENT

EXCERPTS FROM THE U.S. INFANTRY MANUAL:

- Never tell your sergeant you have nothing to do.
- When the pin is pulled, Mr. Grenade is not our friend.
- Bullets don't care if it's dark.
- The quartermaster has two sizes only: Too large and too small.
- A bullet may have your name on it; but shrapnel is addressed to "occupant."
- To remain popular with your buddies, always aim at the enemy.
- Tracers work both ways.
- Remember: If they're in range, so are you.
- When in doubt, empty your magazine.
- Bring as many friends to a gunfight as possible.
- Incoming fire has the right of way.
- Don't draw fire; it irritates the people around you.
- Try to look unimportant; they may be low on ammo.
- Teamwork is essential—it gives the enemy someone else to shoot at.
- If you are in range of a nuclear explosion, advice is superfluous.

. . . never share a foxhole with someone braver than you. - LCG

JUNE

June

June is the sixth month in both the Julian and Gregorian calendars. The Latin name for June is *Iunius*.

Ovid offers multiple etymologies for the name in the *Fasti*, a poem about the Roman calendar. The first is that the month is named after the Roman goddess Juno, the goddess of marriage and the wife of the supreme deity Jupiter; the second is that the name comes from the Latin word *iuniores*, meaning "younger ones", as opposed to *maiores* ("elders") for which the preceding month May *(Maius)* may be named.

In Old English, this month was often referred to as simply "midsummer month." It also may have been called "sere-month," meaning "dry and withered," though this term may have meant June, July, or August.

It wasn't until the seventeenth century, that the Latin name for the sixth month crept into English, *Iūnius*, meaning either "sacred to Juno," or the "younger ones" (at this point in history, the capital forms of J and I were not yet distinguished from one another).

Juno is the Roman counterpart to the Greek goddess Hera. In Roman myth, she is the patron goddess of Rome. She is shown alternately as a cruel goddess (in

Virgil's *Aeneid*) and the goddess of marriage and childbirth. In fact, summer weddings are still very popular, and they may have started because of the blessing that this goddess bestowed on those wed in her sacred month.*

----

*In contrast, the ancient Romans considered the period from mid-May through mid-June inauspicious for marriage. Ovid says that he consulted the *Flaminica Dialis*, the high priestess of Jupiter, about setting a date for his daughter's wedding, and was advised to wait till after June 15. Plutarch, however, implies that the entire month of June was more favorable for weddings than May. - LCG

Thought for Today (June 1)

THE "CELEBRITY BIRTHDAY" DEPARTMENT

"Only the public can make a star. It's the studios who try to make a system out of it." - Marilyn Monroe

Born Norma Jeane Mortenson on June 1, 1926, Marilyn Monroe was famous for playing "dumb blonde" characters and became one of the most popular sex symbols of the 1950s.

Monroe's troubled private life received much attention. She struggled with addiction, depression, and anxiety; and she had highly publicized marriages that ended in divorce.

Marilyn began modeling swimsuits in 1946, which led to her first film in 1947. It was a bit part in the movie, *The Shocking Miss Pilgrim*; however, by 1953, she was one of the most bankable Hollywood stars with leading roles in several films.

Monroe died at her home in Los Angeles on August 5, 1962, from an overdose of barbiturates. She was 36 years old.

"Of the nude pictures: Sure I posed. I needed the money."
- Marilyn Monroe

"They've said I want to direct pictures. I couldn't direct traffic."
- Marilyn Monroe

Thought for Today (June 2)

THE "ENGLISH IS A SECOND LANGUAGE FOR US ALL" DEPARTMENT

"Cleave" is the only English word with two synonyms that are antonyms of each other: adhere and separate.

You should cleave to this thought and not cleave it from your memory (Yeah, I know—that was pretty bad; and you deserve better). I wonder: Is there a synonym for "synonym?" - LCG

Thought for Today (June 3)

THE "DECIDED RELIANCE ON MEDICAL SCIENCE" DEPARTMENT

There's nothing wrong with me that liposuction, LASIK surgery, and a hair transplant can't cure.

– L. C. Gambone

. . . and that does not consider even the benefits of a lobotomy. - LCG

Thought for Today (June 4)

THE "STIRRING STATEMENTS" DEPARTMENT

"In the heart of every man is a desire for a battle to fight, an adventure to live and a beauty to rescue."

- John Eldredge

. . . you forgot beer! - LCG

Thought for Today (June 5)

THE "WORDS TO PONDER" DEPARTMENT

"Regret something you have done, rather than regret something you should have done but didn't."

- Richard Horne

Regretfully, I regret having to regret so many regrets. - LCG

Thought for Today (June 6)

THE "IT'S A WILDE WORLD" DEPARTMENT

"Some cause happiness wherever they go; others whenever they go." - Oscar Wilde (1854-1900)

. . . some cause blissful happiness if they go away forever! - LCG

Thought for Today (June 7)

THE "DEFINITIVE REMARKS" DEPARTMENT

When I was a young man, I was outstanding in my field . . . but, then it rained and I got wet. – L. C. Gambone

---.

. . . and that's why I'm all wet and not just a drip! - LCG

Thought for Today (June 8)

THE "WELL, IT'S ABOUT TIME . . ." DEPARTMENT

On June 8, 1939, King George VI became the first English monarch to visit the United States of America.

In August 1938, President Franklin D. Roosevelt learned that Britain's king and queen were planning a trip to Canada. FDR composed a letter to George VI asking the king to ". . . extend your visit to include the United States."

Three months later, the king wrote back: "I am happy to say that the way now seems clear for me to . . . accept this invitation, which I do with the utmost pleasure."

On the evening of June 7, 1939, the king and queen and their party left Ontario, reaching Washington D.C. by train at 11:00 AM the next morning. Upon his arrival, King George became the first English monarch to visit the United States of America.

No English monarch had set foot in the "new world" prior to 1939. Since then, Queen Elizabeth visited Canada several times and, at the time of this printing, the United States on three occasions, the last being in 2007.

Oh, I say, a jaunt to the colonies would be positively smashing! - LCG

Thought for Today (June 9)

THE "WORDS OF WISDUMB" DEPARTMENT

"Blessed is he who can laugh at himself for he shall never cease to be amused." - Anonymous

---

. . . and now you know why I am always cheerful. - LCG

Thought for Today (June 10)

THE "NOW THIS IS INTERESTING" DEPARTMENT

Aoccdrnig to rscheearch at Cmabrigde Uinervtisy, it deosn't mttaer in waht oredr the ltteers in a wrod are, the olny iprmoetnt tihng is that the frist and lsat ltteer be at the rghit pclae. The rset can be a taotl mses and you can sitll raed it wouthit a porbelm. Tihs is bcuseae the huamn mnid deos not raed ervey lteter by istlef, but the wrod as a wlohe.

. . . It took 20 minutes, you know, to get that stupid paragraph through the stupid spell-checker! - LCG

Thought for Today (June 11)

THE "RIGHT TO THE POINT" DEPARTMENT

"Show me a good loser, and I'll show you a loser."
                                        - Vince Lombardi

Vincent Thomas Lombardi (June 11, 1913 – September 3, 1970) was an Italian-American football player, coach, and executive in the National Football League (NFL). He is best known as the head coach of the Green Bay Packers during the 1960s, where he led the team to three straight and five total NFL Championships in seven years. In addition Lombardi won the first two Super Bowls at the conclusion of the 1966 and 1967 NFL seasons.

Following his death from cancer in 1970, The NFL Super Bowl trophy was named in his honor. He was enshrined in the Pro Football Hall of Fame in 1971, the year after his death. Lombardi is considered by many to be the greatest coach in football history, and more significantly, he is recognized as one of the greatest coaches and leaders in the history of any American sport.

"Perfection is not attainable, but if we chase perfection we can catch excellence." - Vince Lombardi

Thought for Today (June 12)

THE "POLITICAL TRUTH" DEPARTMENT

"Any American who is prepared to run for president should automatically, by definition, be disqualified from ever doing so." - Gore Vidal

---

Gore Vidal for President! . . . . Oh, wait a minute. I just remembered that Mr. Vidal passed away in 2012.

. . . . GORE VIDAL FOR PRESIDENT! - LCG

Thought for Today (June 13)

THE "POLITICAL MANIA" DEPARTMENT

"Politicians are wonderful people as long as they stay away from things they don't understand, such as working for a living." - P. J. O'Rourke

---

I thought about going into politics; however, I'm not unethical, immoral, dishonest, egotistical, and deceitful. In other words, I don't possess the necessary qualifications. - LCG

Thought for Today (June 14)

THE "YOU HEARD IT ON THAT COUNTRY MUSIC STATION" DEPARTMENT

Country and Western music characterizes the experience of living life unlike any other medium. No other musical genre comes even close to portraying life's gritty, down-to-earth, grass roots nature with the verve, the vitality, the sheer energy of Country and Western. If you don't believe me, just "check out" these lyrics:

- "My love for you goes just as deep as your pockets."

- "Put some money in that jukebox, honey. I wanna dance."

- "I got the calf ropin' cow punchin' blues."

- "I ain't drinkin' any more, and I ain't drinkin' any less."

- "I was a square when you were around."

- "I sobered up, and I got to thinkin' . . . . You ain't much fun now that I quit drinkin'."

- "I'm gonna put a bar inside my car and drive myself to drink."

And my all-time favorite,

- "If I shot you sooner, I'd be out of jail by now."

Now, y'all listen up! If this here stuff don't put the gravy on your biscuits each morning, y'all just ain't livin' right!. - LCG

Thought for Today (June 15)

THE "INTERESTING FACTS" DEPARTMENT

EVENTS OF INTEREST THAT OCCURRED JUNE 15:[28]

1215 - King John signed the Magna Carta at Runnymede, near Windsor, England.

1626 - King Charles I disbanded the English Parliament.

1664 - New Jersey was established.

1836 - Arkansas entered the union as the 25th state; its capital is Little Rock and its motto is "Regnat Populus" (The people rule).

1898 - The US House of Representatives accepted the annexation of Hawaii.

1911 - Incorporation of the Tabulating Computing Recording Corporation (later better known as IBM).

1940 - France surrendered to NAZI Germany; German troops occupied Paris.

2002 - Near earth asteroid 2002MN missed the Earth by 75,000 miles (120,000km), about one-third the distance between the Earth and the Moon.

----

[28] https://www.onthisday.com/events/june/15 (accessed 6/17/18)

Thought for Today (June 16)

THE "SAY IT AGAIN, SAM" DEPARTMENT

The Question: "Play it again, Sam"[29] is one of the most famous quoted movie lines in history. In what movie did Humphrey Bogart say, "Play it again, Sam?"

The Answer: According to . . . well, everyone . . . Richard "Rick" Blaine (played by Humphrey Bogart) says, "Play it again, Sam," in the 1942 film classic, *Casablanca.*

But, in actuality, he didn't say it. In fact, nobody said it.

There are two exchanges in *Casablanca* that come close: The first takes place between Ilsa Lund (played by Ingrid Bergman) and Sam (played by Dooley Wilson).

> Ilsa: Play it once, Sam; for old times' sake.
> Sam: [Lying] I don't know what you mean, Miss Ilsa.
> Ilsa: Play it, Sam. Play "As Time Goes By."
> Sam: [Lying] Oh, I can't remember it, Miss Ilsa.
>   I'm a little rusty on it.

---

[29] https://www.infoplease.com/askeds/editing-film-history (accessed 6/17/18)

The second exchange takes place between Rick and Sam.

> Rick: You played it for her; you can play it for me!
> Sam: [Lying] Well, I don't think I can remember . . .
> Rick: If she can stand it, I can! Play it!

In actuality, "Play it again, Sam," is one of the most famous **misquoted** movie lines in history.

AUTHOR'S NOTE: You realize, of course, that Sam had three lines in these dialogues—and he lied all three times. I don't know about you, but I think Sam had a little problem with veracity. - LCG

Well . . . if nobody said it in the movie, then I'll say it right now, right here in print:
Play it again, Sam.

. . . so, the next time someone asks you who said, "Play it again, Sam," you can respond truthfully, "Larry Gambone in his fantastic book *A Thought For Each Day*." - LCG

Thought for Today (June 17)

THE "DEFINITIVE DEFINITIONS" DEPARTMENT

MAD:

"Mad, adj. Affected with a high degree of intellectual independence; not conforming to standards of thought, speech, and action derived by the conformants from study of themselves; at odds with the majority; in short, unusual. It is noteworthy that persons are pronounced mad by officials destitute of evidence that themselves are sane." – Ambrose Bierce

---

. . . and all this time I thought I was just nuts. - LCG

Thought for Today (June 18)

THE "WHY DOESN'T YOUR COMPUTER WORK?" DEPARTMENT

My computer beat me at chess . . .
. . . But I won at kickboxing.

Artificial Intelligence will beat Natural Stupidity every time. - LCG

Thought for Today (June 19)

THE "FOREST FOR THE TREES" DEPARTMENT

If a man speaks in the forest; and there is no woman around to hear him . . . is he still wrong?

If a woman speaks in the forest; and there is no man around to hear her . . . will she still buy shoes?

. . . the answer is a "shoe-in" . . . (I had to say it). - LCG

Thought for Today (June 20)

THE "CLASSICAL QUOTES" DEPARTMENT

"You cannot have a proud and chivalrous spirit if your conduct is mean and paltry."

- Demosthenes (384-322 BCE)

Does anybody use "paltry" anymore? Seriously, don't you think it would sound much more sophisticated if he had said "mean and deplorable" or "mean and despicable?" When I hear the word "paltry" I think of chickens. - LCG

Thought for Today (June 21)

THE "MATERIAL MOTIVATION" DEPARTMENT

"I don't exercise. If God wanted me to bend over, He'd have put diamonds on the floor." - Joan Rivers

----

If God wanted me to bend over, He wouldn't have herniated my discs.
- LCG

Thought for Today (June 22)

THE "UPLIFTING UTTERANCES" DEPARTMENT

I'm always up: I wake up, I look up, I sit up, I get up, I stay up, I keep up, I slip up, I mess up, I pick up, I stack up, I screw up, I give up, I drink up, I throw up, I clean up . . . .

. . . I'm fed up.

- L. C. Gambone

. . . I come up . . . with the dumbest sayings . . . . - LCG

Thought for Today (June 23)

THE "MORE MOVIE MISQUOTES" DEPARTMENT

Badges?

A little while back I provided you with the true story behind the movie quote, "Play it again, Sam." Today's "Thought" will delve into another famous movie quote.

The Question: What movie does the legendary quote, "Badges? We don't need no stinkin' badges,"[30] come from?

The Answer: "Badges? We don't need no stinkin' badges!" is a line of dialogue that is quoted widely from the 1948 film, *The Treasure of the Sierra Madre*. Unfortunately, similar to "Play it again, Sam," the line is a misquote.

The line was derived from dialogue in a 1927 novel, *The Treasure of the Sierra Madre*, written by B. Traven, which was the basis for the movie. The original line (in the book) contained English and Spanish profanities, which, because of the Hays Commission, were removed for the film.

So, in the film, a Mexican bandit leader named "Gold Hat" (portrayed by Alfonso Bedoya) tries to convince Fred C.

---

[30] https://en.wikipedia.org/wiki/Stinking_badges (accessed 6/17/18)

Dobbs (played by Humphrey Bogart) that he and his company are *Federales*.

What follows is the actual dialogue from the film:

DOBBS: If you're the police, then where are your badges?

GOLD HAT: Badges? We ain't got no badges. We don't need no badges. I don't have to show you any stinkin' badges!*

Though Bedoya comes close, he never says in actuality, "We don't need no stinkin' badges." It is a misquote that comes from several sources, the most prominent being the 1974 movie *Blazing Saddles*, and a 1967 episode of the TV series, *The Monkees*. - LCG

---

*In 2005, the full quote from the film was chosen as number 36 on the American Film Institute list, *AFI's 100 Years...100 Movie Quotes*. - LCG

Thought for Today (June 24)

THE "TO DRINK, OR NOT TO DRINK" DEPARTMENT

I'm on a whisky diet . . . I've lost three days already!

- Tommy Cooper

My wife wanted me to go on a salmon diet . . . sounded fishy to me (go ahead and groan). If you want better one-liners, you'll have to pay more for the book. - LCG

Thought for Today (June 25)

THE "INTERESTING FACTS" DEPARTMENT

On June 25 . . .[31]

The Lunar eclipse in 1638 is the 1st astronomical event recorded in the American Colonies.

Virginia, the 10th state, entered the Union in 1788. Its capital is Richmond, and its motto is "Sic Semper Tyrannis" (Thus Always to Tyrants).

US President Andrew Johnson passes a law in 1868 that government workers would work an 8-hour day.

The Battle of the Little Bighorn was fought in 1876. A unit of the 7th Cavalry under Lieutenant Colonel George Armstrong Custer was wiped out by Sioux and Cheyenne warriors.

The Korean conflict began in 1950 when North Korean troops invaded South Korea.

. . . a state, a battle, a war, an eclipse, and an 8-hour work day . . . . all on June 25! - LCG

---

[31] https://www.onthisday.com/events/june/25 (accessed 6/17/18)

Thought for Today (June 26)

THE "DEFINITELY ON BOARD" DEPARTMENT

BOARDWALKS

New Jersey is the location of most of the boardwalks in the United States. Nearly every town and city along the Jersey Shore has at least one boardwalk with various attractions.[32]

The world's oldest boardwalk opened in Atlantic City, New Jersey, on June 26, 1870. It was 1 mile (1.6 km) long and 8 feet (2.4 meters) wide. Its purpose was to reduce the amount of sand tracked into local businesses.

The boardwalk grew to 7 miles (11 km) in length, stretching from Atlantic City to Longport, New Jersey, before it was destroyed in the great 1944 hurricane that ravaged the Jersey Shore.

Today, although partially destroyed once again in 2012 by hurricane Sandy, it is 5.5 miles (8.8 km) long—including 1.5 miles (2.4 km) in Ventnor, NJ—making it not only the oldest, but one of the longest boardwalks in the world.

I hope I haven't bored you with this boardwalk tale. - LCG

---

[32] https://en.wikipedia.org/wiki/Boardwalk (accessed 6/17/18)

Thought for Today (June 27)

THE "SHOULD HAVE QUIT BEFORE STARTING" DEPARTMENT

"If 'Winners Never Quit and Quitters Never Win' . . .
then what fool came up with 'Quit While You're Ahead?'"

- Anonymous

Do smokers win if they quit? - LCG

Thought for Today (June 28)

THE "TO DRINK, OR NOT TO DRINK" DEPARTMENT

The Greek historian, Herodotus (484-425 BCE), writes in Book I, chapter 133, of his *Histories*, that the ancient Persians decided upon important matters by debating the decision first while drunk and then, the next day, while sober.

He states also that they did the opposite: If their initial decision was made while sober, they made their final decision while drunk.

If Congress got drunk on booze instead of power, the decisions would still be bad, but at least the members would get along (hopefully). - LCG

Thought for Today (June 29)

THE "YOU READ IT IN TRAFFIC" DEPARTMENT

BUMPER STICKERS:

MAKE LOVE NOT WAR

. . . GET MARRIED AND DO BOTH.

OUTSOURCE CONGRESS!

IF YOU DON'T LIKE THE WAY I DRIVE,

GET OFF THE SIDEWALK!

BE YOURSELF . . . .

NO ONE ELSE WANTS THE JOB.

BUMPER STICKER: I drive way too fast to worry about cholesterol! - LCG

Thought for Today (June 30)

THE "AUTOMOTIVE HISTORY" DEPARTMENT

CHEVROLET CORVETTE

The first generation Chevrolet Corvette was introduced as a show car for the 1953 Motorama display at the New York Auto Show.[33] The vehicle generated enough interest to induce GM to make a production version to sell to the public.

Only 300 hand-built polo-white Corvette convertibles were built for the 1953 production year. The first car rolled off the assembly line on June 30, 1953.

Myron Scott, the creator of the All-American Soap Box Derby, is credited for naming the car after a type of small, maneuverable warship called a corvette. Originally, the Corvette was built in Flint, Michigan and St. Louis, Missouri; however, since 1981, the Corvette has been manufactured in Bowling Green, Kentucky and is the official sports car of the Commonwealth of Kentucky.

. . . I searched on line and found a 1953 Corvette convertible in mint condition for sale . . . you had to register with the broker to see the price (yeah, right!). - LCG

---

[33] https://en.wikipedia.org/wiki/Chevrolet_Corvette (accessed 6/17/18)

Lawrence C. Gambone

JULY

July

In both the Julian and Gregorian calendars, July is the seventh month of the year (between June and August). It is the fourth month to have the length of 31 days.

In the original Roman ten-month calendar, the month was named, *Quintilis*, which means Fifth Month. It became the seventh month around 450 BCE (but retained its name). Finally, in 45 BCE, *Quintilis* was renamed "July" (Latin *Iulius*) by the Roman Senate in honor of Roman general Julius Caesar, who was born on the 13th day of the month in 100 BCE.

Lawrence C. Gambone

Thought for Today (July 1)

THE "PREPOSTEROUS POLITICAL POLEMICS" DEPARTMENT

"Politics is the art of looking for trouble, finding it everywhere, diagnosing it incorrectly and applying the wrong remedies." - Groucho Marx

---

. . . and judging by today's political state of affairs, this is an on-going process that has not changed. - LCG

Thought for Today (July 2)

THE "PROMISING POLITICAL POLEMICS" DEPARTMENT

"I believe all politicians should be restricted to two terms: One in office and one in prison."

— Practically Everybody

. . . and that's what I call "political expediency." - LCG

Thought for Today (July 3)

THE "CELEBRATE INDEPENDENCE" DEPARTMENT

In honor of the coming Independence Day holiday:

The Nine Capitals of the United States

Before establishing Washington, D.C. as the permanent seat of government, Congress has met in nine locations since it first convened in Philadelphia in 1774. Without searching the internet (or reading ahead), can you name the nine locations?

(The answer will be furnished in tomorrow's "Thought for Today.")

"Ours is the only country deliberately founded on a good idea."
- John Gunther

Thought for Today (July 4)

THE "CELEBRATE INDEPENDENCE" DEPARTMENT

In Honor of Independence Day:

AUTHOR'S NOTE: As promised, and with great thanks to my friend, Andy Butrica, for providing me with the historical facts, here is the answer to the July 3 "Thought For Today" that asked if you knew the Nine Capitals of the United States.

- LCG

The Nine Capitals of the United States

Since it first convened in Philadelphia in 1774, and until establishing Washington, D.C. as the permanent seat of government, Congress has met in nine locations.

The first and second "Continental Congresses" met in Philadelphia in 1774. So did the 1787 constitutional convention. However, during the Revolutionary War, the British occupied Philadelphia, forcing Congress to relocate, which it did—several times, in fact—to various cities and towns throughout the colonies: Baltimore and Annapolis in Maryland; York and Lancaster in Pennsylvania; Princeton and Trenton in New Jersey.

In 1783, in recognition of Mr. Mason's and Mr. Dixon's sectional division of the Union (north vs. south), Congress decided to have two capitals: one on the Delaware River near Trenton, New Jersey, and the other on the Potomac. A year later Congress voted to establish a single federal town near Trenton and to meet in New York City until buildings at the newly designated capital were completed.

Southerners blocked appropriations for the construction in Trenton. Consequently, Congress remained in New York City despite repeated efforts by both Pennsylvanians and Southerners to bring it back to Philadelphia, the original seat of Congress from 1774 to 1783. In the meantime, Annapolis, Baltimore, and even Lancaster, Pennsylvania, competed against New York City for the "honor" of being the nation's capital.

Late in August 1789, Congress once again took up the question of locating the federal capital. After a bitter debate between representatives from north and south of the Mason-Dixon Line, the House agreed to a bill retaining New York City as the temporary residence and locating the permanent capital on the Susquehanna River in Pennsylvania. Most representatives expected Wright's Ferry, renamed Columbia in 1788, to be the specific site. Instead the Senate named Germantown, Pennsylvania, a small town seven miles north of Philadelphia. The bill was tabled at the last minute.

Finally, in 1790, Congress passed the "Residence Act," which moved the federal government to its permanent Potomac River site. Philadelphia became the temporary residence of the capital for the next 10 years until the final relocation in 1800.

So, all in all, "Congress" has met in the following cities and locations:

- Philadelphia, in that old brick building with the bell
- Baltimore, Maryland
- Lancaster, Pennsylvania
- York, Pennsylvania
- Princeton, New Jersey
- Annapolis, Maryland
- Trenton, New Jersey
- Federal Hall, New York City, 1789-1790
- Congress Hall, Philadelphia, 1790-1800
- Washington, DC, from 1800 to the present, though in a variety of buildings.

- Lawrence C. Gambone

Information provided by: Andrew J. Butrica, Ph.D., Historical Consultant

Thought for Today (July 5)

THE "CELEBRATE INDEPENDENCE" DEPARTMENT

In Honor of Independence Day:

This is the final installment to the saga of the Nine Capitals of the United States. If you will remember, I explained that since it first convened in Philadelphia in 1774, Congress has met in nine locations.

Congress "pulled up stakes" and shifted to six of these locations during the Revolutionary War because the British occupied the original capital, Philadelphia. It is interesting to note, however, that during the war, Congress never met in three of America's six largest cities: Charles Town (now Charleston), South Carolina; Savannah, Georgia; and Boston, Massachusetts (the second-largest city during the war).

Most likely, these cities weren't utilized by Congress because, except for Boston, they were occupied by the British throughout most of the war. Three of the largest cities, New York, Baltimore, and Philadelphia, of course, did serve as temporary residences for Congress (although New York, which was occupied by the British, did not become one of the capital cities until after the war).

<u>Boston, Massachusetts:</u> The country's second-largest city at the start of the revolution was eclipsed in population by New York by the end of the war. While Bostonians

may believe their city was the center of the revolution (if not the entire universe), the only events of significance that took place there during the quest for independence were the wanton destruction of some perfectly good tea in Boston Harbor followed by a significant defeat at the battle of Breed's/Bunker Hill.

In all fairness, I should point out that General George Washington laid siege to Boston in March 1776 and forced the British to evacuate. It was one of Washington's few—very few—successful campaigns.

New York, New York: Fresh from his victory in Boston, George Washington traveled to New York where, in August 1776, he undertook what became known as the Battle of Long Island (also known as the Battle of Brooklyn or the Battle of Brooklyn Heights). Unlike Boston, Washington's Continental Army was defeated by a large force of British regulars commanded by General William Howe.

Howe made preparations to conduct a siege; however, Washington evacuated his entire army to Manhattan. Eventually, General .Howe drove the Continental Army out of New York entirely, and the strategically important city fell under British control. In terms of troop size, the Battle of Long Island was the largest battle of the Revolutionary War.

Baltimore, Maryland: No major Battles of the Revolutionary War occurred in Maryland; however, Baltimore served as the temporary capital of the colonies when the Second Continental Congress met there briefly during the period December 1776 to February 1777.

Savannah, Georgia: In 1778, a force of 3,100 British regulars under the command of Lieutenant Colonel Archibald Campbell captured Savannah. The force was dispatched from New York by Lieutenant General Sir Henry Clinton, the commander-in-chief of the British forces. Clinton's plan was to capture Savannah to begin the process of returning Georgia to British control.

While awaiting troops from Florida under the command of Brigadier General Augustine Prevost, Campbell assessed that the American defenses were comparatively weak, and decided to attack without Prevost. He flanked the American position outside the town, captured a large portion of Major General Robert Howe's army, and routed the remnants, who retreated into South Carolina. In 1779, the British resisted a siege by a combined force of French and American soldiers and held the city until late in the war.

Charleston, South Carolina: The battle for Charleston in 1780, resulted in America's worst defeat of the war. With the surrender of Charleston, the British captured more than 3,000 rebel troops and a great quantity of munitions and equipment.

In an ironic "twist of fate," the long-term results of Charleston's capture were favorable for the Americans. Confident of British control in the South, Lieutenant General Sir Henry Clinton sailed north to New York after the victory, leaving General Charles Cornwallis in command of 8,300 British forces in the South. Lacking Clinton's support, Cornwallis surrendered to George Washington a little over a year later at Yorktown, Virginia.

<u>Philadelphia, Pennsylvania:</u> This was the nation's largest city during the revolution; and in my opinion it is (should be) the true capital of the United States. Although many believe the concept of independence, and even the Revolutionary War itself, may have started in Boston (actually the war started in Lexington, about 14 miles outside of Boston); it cannot be denied that the definitive concept of an "independent nation" took hold in Philadelphia.

The following three important documents affected the history of the United States—indeed, the entire world. All three were conceived and signed in Philadelphia.

The Declaration of Independence;

The Articles of Confederation (the nation's first attempt to unify); and

The Constitution of the United States of America (including, subsequently, The Bill of Rights).

- Lawrence C. Gambone

God Bless America! - LCG

Thought for Today (July 6)

THE "GOOD GOD IT'S GOVERNMENT" DEPARTMENT

"The mystery of government is not how Washington works but how to make it stop." - P. J. O'Rourke

---

. . . government, unfortunately, can be stopped only by another government. - LCG

Thought for Today (July 7)

THE "OBVIOUSLY STATING THE OBVIOUS" DEPARTMENT

Education requires intelligence, diligence, and perseverance.

Success requires dedication, determination, and hard work.

Stupid is easy!

- Lawrence C. Gambone

. . . and I always take the easy route. - LCG

Thought for Today (July 8)

THE "YOU KNOW YOU HEARD IT HERE FIRST" DEPARTMENT

"Even more exasperating than the guy who thinks he knows it all is the one who really does." - Al Bernstein

---

. . . my grandkids (just like my kids) are convinced they know it all; there's no thinking involved. - LCG

Thought for Today (July 9)

THE "YOU READ IT ON THE ROAD" DEPARTMENT

BUMPER STICKER:

> SAVE THE EARTH . . . .
>
> IT'S THE ONLY PLANET WITH CHOCOLATE.

Etymologists believe the origin of the word "chocolate" may be from the *Nahuatl* (Aztec) word "*xocoatl*," which means, "bitter water." It referred to a bitter drink the Aztecs brewed from cacao beans. The Latin name for the cacao tree is, *Theobroma cacao.* - LCG

Thought for Today (July 10)

THE "INTERESTING FACTS" DEPARTMENT

EVENTS OF INTEREST THAT OCCURRED JULY 10:[34]

988 - The city of Dublin was founded on the banks of the river Liffey.

1040 - Lady Godiva allegedly rode naked through Coventry to force her husband, the Earl of Mercia, to lower taxes.

1212 - The most severe of several early fires burned most of London to the ground.

1778 - American Revolution: Louis XVI of France declared war on the Kingdom of Great Britain.

1890 – Wyoming, the 44th state entered the Union. Its capital is Cheyenne, and its motto is "Equal Rights."

1892 - 1st concrete-paved street was built in Bellefountaine, Ohio.

1913 - Death Valley, California hit 134 °F (56.7 °C), the highest temperature recorded in the United States.

---

[34] https://www.onthisday.com/events/july/10 (accessed 6/17/18)

1918 - Russian Soviet Federal Socialist Republic formed.

1940 – The Battle of Britain began as Nazi forces attacked shipping convoys in the English Channel.

1943 - US, British, and Canadian forces invaded Sicily in WW II (Operation Husky).

1962 - Telstar, the 1st geosynchronous communications satellite, was launched.

1965 – The Beatles' "VI" album became #1 and stayed #1 for 6 weeks.

1965 - Rolling Stones scored their 1st US #1 single "(I Can't Get No) Satisfaction."

2005 - Hurricane Dennis slammed into the Florida Panhandle causing billions of dollars in damage.

Thought for Today (July 11)

THE "WRIGHT IS NEVER WRONG" DEPARTMENT

"I used to be indecisive. Now I'm not sure."

- Steven Wright

. . . Could you be a little more definitive about this, Steve? - LCG

Thought for Today (July 12)

THE "ABSOLUTE WORST JOKES EVER" DEPARTMENT

Two peanuts walk into a rowdy bar.
One was assaulted.

A jumper cable walks into a bar.
The barman says, "I'll serve you, but don't start anything."

A sandwich walks into a bar.
The barman says, "Sorry, we don't serve food in here."

A man walks into a bar with a slab of asphalt under his arm and says, "Gimme a beer; and one for the road."

A dyslexic man walks into a bra . . . .

Two antennae meet on a roof, fall in love and get married.
The ceremony wasn't much, but the reception was great.

Two cannibals are eating a clown.
One says to the other, "Does this taste funny to you?"

Two cows are standing next to each other in a field.
Daisy says to Dolly, "I was artificially inseminated this morning."
"I don't believe you," said Dolly.
"It's true," Daisy replied. "No bull!"

Two hydrogen atoms meet.
One says, "I've lost my electron."
The other says, "Are you sure?"
The first replies, "Yes, I'm positive."

A man takes his Rottweiler to the vet and says, "My dog's cross-eyed. Is there anything you can do for him?"
"Well," says the vet, "let's have a look at him."
So, he picks the dog up and examines his eyes, checks his teeth, etc. Finally, he says, "I'm going to have to put him down."
"What? Just because he's cross-eyed?"
"No, because he's really, really heavy."

I went to a seafood disco last week . . . and pulled a mussel.

Two Eskimos sitting in a kayak were chilly, and when they lit a fire in the craft, it sank. This proves that you can't have your kayak and heat it, too.

The banana said to the melon, "Let's run away and get married."
The melon replied, "I'm sorry, but I cantaloupe."

If a joke is so bad it makes you laugh . . . is it a good joke?

Hey . . . I warned you that the jokes were bad! - LCG

Thought for Today (July 13)

THE "DEFINITIVE DEFINITIONS" DEPARTMENT

"Criminal: A person with predatory instincts who has not sufficient capital to form a corporation." - Howard Scott

---

I believe that says it all. - LCG

Thought for Today (July 14)

THE "FACETIOUS FELINES" DEPARTMENT

"Cats are smarter than dogs. You can't get eight cats to pull a sled through snow." - Jeff Valdez

---

Heck . . . you can't get eight cats to do anything! - LCG

Thought for Today (July 15)

THE "ENGLISH IS A SECOND LANGUAGE FOR US ALL" DEPARTMENT

INFINITIVES: To split; or not to split? That is the question.

While writing my first book,[35] I was berated by my editor for splitting infinitives. Apparently I did it so often that, finally, he stated emphatically, "That's the last one I'm going to point out; you find and fix the rest!"

It seems I had broken repeatedly the ages-old law of English grammar that decried splitting the "to verb;" and as a result of his tirade, I fixed my offending "adverbial insertions," and in the process, became a rabid, fervent "anti-infinitive-splitter." However, the question becomes: is splitting infinitives an ages-old law? In fact, is it a law indeed?

Apparently not. I researched "split infinitive" and found that, though injunctions against "splitting" may have been implied earlier, it wasn't until 1864 that Henry Alford, the Dean of Canterbury, introduced the idea formally that an adverb should not be placed in the middle of an infinitive.[36] He did this in his book, *The Queen's English*. However, Alford did not state it as a rule; rather he

---

[35] *Why Corporations Fail*, available on Amazon.com.

[36] Alford may have been influenced by the fact that Latin infinitives, as well as infinitives in many languages, are single words: for example "to go" and "to speak" in French are *aller* and *parler*, respectively.

stated merely that he saw "no good reason" to split the infinitive. He supported his supposition by proclaiming, ". . . this practice is entirely unknown to English speakers and writers."

Nevertheless, though Alford suggested nothing stronger than "no good reason" to split the "to verb;" somehow grammarians and teachers in America and Great Britain began hammering the *de facto* concept as if it were a *de jure* standard. In effect, if it didn't become law, it became a commandment: Thou shalt split not thy infinitives.

In the 1906 book, *The King's English*, the brothers Henry W. Fowler and Francis G. Fowler pronounced the split infinitive "ugly;" nevertheless, they believed also that the "prohibitions had gone too far." The Fowlers wrote, ". . . instead of warning the novice against splitting his infinitives, we must warn him against the curious superstition that the splitting or not splitting makes the difference between a good and a bad writer."

In fact, many respected writers, both before and after the times of Alford and the Fowlers, have employed split infinitives, including (to name a few) Thomas Cromwell, Daniel Defoe, Lord Byron, F. Scott Fitzgerald, Elizabeth Gaskell, Benjamin Franklin, Samuel Johnson, and Elizabeth Barrett Browning. Some consider Byron to be the father of the split infinitive: "To slowly trace," wrote the noble poet, "the forest's shady scene."

Finally, the *Chicago Manual of Style* (the undisputed book-writer's bible) frowned on the split infinitive until its thirteenth edition (1983). The sixteenth edition, in paragraphs 5.103 and 5.168, suggests that it is ok to split an infinitive when the intervening adverb is used for emphasis (a fact my editor bemoans vociferously).

Thus, according to the latest edition of the Chicago manual, "to boldly go where no man has gone before," undeniably the most famous split infinitive of the 20th century, actually may be ok. Personally, I don't think so. I agree with the Fowler brothers. I think it is ugly; and were I to write it, I would state, ". . . to go boldly where no man has gone before." Or, perhaps, I would employ a gerund: ". . . boldly going where no man has gone before."

To sum it up: Until rather recently, generations of school children and novice writers (myself having occupied both categories) were taught that splitting an infinitive is taboo. However, in the English language, the infinitive is composed of two words. Therefore, you could argue that English infinitives are *always* split—by a space—and whether you are permitted to stick something in that space or not may be moot.

– Lawrence C. Gambone

I think I have to rethink what I think I thought about infinitives. - LCG

Thought for Today (July 16)

THE "PORTENTOUS POLITICAL POLEMICS" DEPARTMENT

Placing the Ten Commandments in a building full of politicians would create a hostile work environment.

. . . Thou shalt not . . . What! - LCG

Thought for Today (July 17)

THE "WORDS OF WISDUMB" DEPARTMENT

I would be quite content to live on my past glory, but . . . as my wife reminds me constantly . . . I did nothing glorious in my past. - L. C. Gambone

----

I drink; therefore, I could be. - LCG

Thought for Today (July 18)

THE "LANGUAGE LUNACY" DEPARTMENT

The troops received their just deserts after dessert and began to desert into the desert.

Another example of why English is "a second language for us all." - LCG

Thought for Today (July 19)

THE "BETCHA DIDN'T KNOW THAT" DEPARTMENT

The word "**boondocks**" (and its contraction "boonies") is an American expression that referred originally to a remote rural area, but now is applied often to an out-of-the-way city or town considered to be backward and unsophisticated.

"Boondocks" was introduced to English at the beginning of the 20th Century by U.S. military personnel serving in the Philippines. The expression derives from the Tagalog word "*bundok,*" which means "mountain." In the Philippines, since most major cities and settlements are located on or near the coastline, the word *bundok* is also a colloquialism referring to rural inland areas, which are usually mountainous and difficult to access.

. . . so, English took another foreign word and made it "English." - LCG

Thought for Today (July 20)

THE "MILITARY TRADITIONS" DEPARTMENT

Medieval knights raised their visors to identify themselves to the king—the origin of the modern military salute.

More trivia from yours truly . . . on a "neat to know" basis. - LCG

Thought for Today (July 21)

THE "KEEP IT COOL" DEPARTMENT

Be enthusiastic, even if people think you're uncool —
they'll think you equally uncool if you are aloof or cynical.

. . . maybe they think you're uncool because you ARE uncool. - LCG

Thought for Today (July 22)

THE "INTERESTING FACTS" DEPARTMENT

EVENTS OF INTEREST THAT OCCURRED JULY 22:[37]

1099 - First Crusade: Godfrey of Bouillon is elected the
first Defender of the Holy Sepulcher of The
Kingdom of Jerusalem.

1587 - 2nd English colony forms on Roanoke Island off
North Carolina.

1686 - City of Albany, NY chartered.

1775 - George Washington takes command of the
Continental Army.

---

[37] https://www.onthisday.com/events/july/22 (accessed 6/17/18)

1793 – Alexander Mackenzie reaches the Pacific Ocean becoming the first person to complete a transcontinental crossing of Canada.

1796 – Cleveland, Ohio, founded by Gen Moses Cleveland.

1893 – Katharine Lee Bates writes "America the Beautiful" in Colorado.

1939 – Jane Bolin becomes the 1st African American female judge (NY).

1943 – US forces led by Gen George Patton liberate Palermo Sicily.

1963 – The Beatles release "Introducing the Beatles."

1975 – US House of Representatives votes to restore citizenship to General Robert E. Lee.

1994 – O.J. Simpson pleads "Absolutely 100% Not Guilty" of murder.

2015 – "Oldest" Qur'an fragments discovered; radiocarbon testing dates to 568 - 645 CE.

. . . It's the facts, ma'am, just the facts. - LCG

Thought for Today (July 23)

THE "CONCEPTS TO CONSIDER" DEPARTMENT

"Remember that happiness is a way of travel—not a destination." - Roy M. Goodman

---

. . . so, how come most people ain't happy 'till they get there? I mean doesn't every kid in a car drone constantly, "Are we there, yet?" - LCG

Thought for Today (July 24)

THE "NEVER THOUGHT ABOUT IT THAT WAY" DEPARTMENT

"Well, if crime fighters fight crime and fire fighters fight fire, what do freedom fighters fight? They never mention that part to us, do they?" - George Carlin

---

George Denis Patrick Carlin (May 12, 1937 - June 22, 2008) was an American stand-up comedian, actor, author, and social critic. Carlin was noted for his black comedy and reflections on politics, the English language, psychology, religion, and various taboo subjects. - LCG

Thought for Today (July 25)

THE "RULES AND REGULATIONS" DEPARTMENT

"I believe in rules. If there weren't any rules, how could you break them?" - Leo Durocher

---

. . . I can find a way; I've broken rules BEFORE they were rules. - LCG

Thought for Today (July 26)

THE "GBS" DEPARTMENT

"A life spent making mistakes is not only more honorable, but more useful than a life spent doing nothing."

- George Bernard Shaw

Born in Dublin on July 26, 1856, George Bernard Shaw[38] was an Irish playwright, critic, and polemicist whose influence on Western theatre, culture, and politics extended from the 1880s to his death and beyond. He wrote more than sixty plays, including major works such as *Man and Superman* (1902), *Pygmalion* (1912), and *Saint Joan* (1923). Incorporating both contemporary satire and historical allegory, Shaw became the leading dramatist of his generation, and in 1925 was awarded the Nobel Prize in Literature.

Often Shaw expressed views that were contentious; he promoted eugenics[39] and alphabet reform, and opposed vaccination and organized religion. He courted unpopularity by denouncing both sides in the First World War as equally culpable; and castigated British policy on Ireland in the postwar period. By the late 1920s he often wrote and spoke favorably of dictatorships of the

---

[38] https://en.wikipedia.org/wiki/George_Bernard_Shaw (accessed 6/17/18)

[39] EUGENICS: A set of beliefs and practices directed towards improving the genetic quality of the human population.

right and left—he expressed admiration for both Mussolini and Stalin.

In 1938 he provided the screenplay for a filmed version of *Pygmalion* for which he received an Academy Award.

In the final decade of his life he made fewer public statements, refused all state honors including the Order of Merit in 1946, but continued to write prolifically until shortly before his death on November 2, 1950 at age ninety-four. Since his death, scholarly and critical opinion has varied about his works, but he has been rated regularly as second only to Shakespeare among English-language dramatists.

. . . I Shaw hope you liked this stuff about George. - LCG

Thought for Today (July 27)

THE "SHORT ATTENTION SPAN" DEPARTMENT

"The average attention span of the modern human being is about half as long as whatever you're trying to tell them." - Meg Rosoff

----

People tell me I have a short attention span; but, it's not . . . . oh, look, a puppy. - LCG

Thought for Today (July 28)

THE "NOW YOU KNOW" DEPARTMENT

MOON'S DAY . . . or Why is Monday Called Monday?

The English noun "Monday" derived sometime before 1200 from *monedæi*, which itself developed around 1000 from Old English *mōnandæg* and *mōndæg* (literally meaning "moon's day"). In some cultures Monday is the first day of the week. The Western-Christian tradition held the first day of the week to be the Sabbath (Sunday), which placed Monday as the second day.[40] The Latin term for Monday is *lunae dies* ("day of the moon"). The association of the days of the week with the Sun, the Moon, the gods, and the five planets visible to the naked eye dates to the Roman Empire (2nd century).

The Romans traditionally used a "market week" or eight-day *nundinal* cycle,[41] marked as A to H in the calendar. A *nundinum* was the market day. However, after the Julian calendar had come into effect in 45 BCE, the seven-day week came into use, coexisting with the *nundinal* cycle until adopted officially by Constantine in 321 CE.

---

[40] However, Monday is often considered the first day of the "work week."

[41] Borrowed most likely from the Etruscans, the *nundinal* cycle, market week, or 8-day week (Latin: *nundinum* or *internundinum*) was the cycle of days marked using *nundinal* letters from A to H. The earliest form of the Roman calendar included 38 such cycles, running for 304 days from March to December followed by an unorganized expanse of 50 winter days. The lengths of the Republican and Julian calendars, however, were not evenly divisible by 8; under these systems, the *nundinae* fell on a different letter each year.

Thought for Today (July 29)

THE "THEY SHOULD TABLE THIS PERIODICALLY" DEPARTMENT

If on the Periodic Table of Elements:

Bismuth = Bi
Gadolinium = Gd
Helium = He
Sodium = Na
Yttrium = Y

Then:

$$(Sodium)^4 + (Sodium)^4 + (Helium + Yttrium)^3$$

$$+ (Gadolinium + Bismuth) =$$

Na Na Na Na   Na Na Na Na   HeY HeY HeY   GdBi

. . . better living through chemistry. - LCG

Thought for Today (July 30)

THE "MORNING MOTIVATION" DEPARTMENT

"Each morning I look at the obituary column. If I'm not in it, I go to work." - A. E. Matthews

----

. . . I agree, if I was in it, I'd take the day off, too? - LCG

Thought for Today (July 31)

THE "SONGS WE'D LIKE TO HEAR" DEPARTMENT

OFFICIAL THEME SONGS

"Fools Rush In" — Democratic Party

"Send in the Clowns" — Republican Party

"The Circus is in Town" — U.S. Congress

"Reality" is life . . . with no background music. - LCG

AUGUST

August

Originally, August was called *Sextilis* in Latin because it was the sixth month of the ten-month Roman calendar (March was the first month of the year). It became the eighth month of the year when January and February were added by King Numa Pompilius in 713 BCE. Pompilius gave *Sextilis* 29 days. Julius Caesar added two days when he created the Julian Calendar in 45 BCE, giving *Sextilis* its modern length of 31 days.

In 8 BCE, *Sextilis* was renamed *Augustus* in honor of Octavian Augustus Caesar, Julius Caesar's nephew, who became Rome's first emperor after defeating Marc Anthony and Cleopatra at the battle of Actium in 31 BCE. According to a *Senatus consultum* (a text emanating from the senate in ancient Rome), Augustus chose this month because it was the time of several of his great triumphs, including the conquest of Egypt.

The original Latin name for August was *sextilis mensis* (sixth month), and the Middle English (Anglo-Saxon) name for August was *Weod Monath* (weed month). However, the current designation, August, derives from the later Latin *Augustus mensis* (month of August).

Thought for Today (August 1)

THE "WHATEVER WHENEVER" DEPARTMENT

If you can't be kind, at least
have the decency to be vague.

. . . does issuing a "vague threat" comply with the above? - LCG

Thought for Today (August 2)

THE "IS THIS UPLIFTING OR WHAT?" DEPARTMENT

There are three things you cannot recover in life:

A WORD after it is said, a MOMENT after it is missed, and TIME after it has passed.

. . . yeah, and MONEY after it is spent. - LCG

Thought for Today (August 3)

THE "WHAT'S IN A NAME?" DEPARTMENT

The Generic Sun And Moon

In 1919, an international group of astronomers formed the International Astronomical Union (IAU) for the purpose of naming celestial bodies. As a result, stars have proper names (for example: Polaris, Orion, and Betelgeuse); and likewise, the solar system's many moons (examples: Jupiter's Io, Ganymede, and Europa).

Nevertheless, our sun, although it is a star, doesn't have a unique, proper name in the English language; English speakers just call it "the sun." The Moon, on the other hand, does have a proper name. It has been designated officially by the IAU as . . . uh, well . . . the Moon.

THE SUN[42]

We call it the "sun;" but, according to the International Astronomical Union, no proper or official name has been designated for our solar system's star.

The ancient Greek sun god was, *Helios*; and likewise, the Greeks gave that name to the sun. *Helios* is the root for words such as heliotropic and heliocentric. But, the more commonly used root name for the sun is the Latin word *Sol*, the Roman sun god equivalent to the Greek god *Helios*. It is from *Sol* that the words solar, solarium, and solstice are derived.

---

[42] http://earthsky.org/space/what-is-the-suns-name (accessed 6/17/18)

The first cited use of *Sol* as a proper name for the sun is the 1450 manuscript, "Treatise on Astrology," which is located in the Ashmolean Museum in Oxford, England, and which states: "Sol is hote & dry but not as mars is."

But what about the word "sun?" According to the IAU, neither "*Sol*" nor "sun" are recognized as the sun's proper names. In fact, no one knows for sure how "sun" came to be used. It comes from the Old English word *sunne*, which derives from the Proto-Germanic word *sunnon* (and there are many cognates in other languages such as the Dutch word *zon* and the German *sonne*).

Nevertheless, the IAU has suggested that we capitalize Sun (as if it were a proper name), rather than use the lowercase sun. The result? Confusion: The media generally does not capitalize the word; however, most astronomers do (along with other non-standard capitalizations such as Galaxy, Solar System, and Universe).

THE MOON[43]

Naming the Moon "the Moon" was one of the first things the IAU did when it was formed in 1919 because it wanted "to standardize the multiple, confusing systems of nomenclature for the Moon that were then in use."

The ancient Greeks called the Moon *Selene* and the Romans called it *Luna* (each representing a goddess); but, the word "moon" is not derived from either word. "Moon"

---

[43] https://futurism.com/the-moons-real-name-and-others-too/ (accessed 6/17/18)

can be traced back to Old English. It is believed to come from the Proto-Germanic word "*menon*," which in turn derived from the Proto-Indo-European "*menses*," meaning "month" or "moon."

When adopting the Moon's rather "less-than-spectacular" name, the IAU stated that the Moon was the first known moon, and popularly called something like "the Moon" in many languages for millennia. Therefore, it was easier to make the name official than to introduce a new name (the IAU's goal, after all, was to make things easier for people to understand, not harder).

IN SUMMATION

According to the International Astronomical Union, the Moon has a proper, albeit generic, name; the sun does not. But, I ask: Shouldn't the sun be named properly "the Sun?" After all, employing the IAU's logic, the sun was the first known sun; and, no doubt popularly was called something like "the sun" in many languages for millennia.

. . . I wonder: Was the sun out when the IAU mooned us? - LCG

Lawrence C. Gambone

Thought for Today (August 4)

THE "TWO PLUS TWO EQUALS . . . UH?" DEPARTMENT

"The different branches of Arithmetic — Ambition, Distraction, Uglification, and Derision." - Lewis Carroll

----

. . . and all this time I thought they were Amnesia, Dissention, Mixology, and Dementia. - LCG

Thought for Today (August 5)

THE "LESSONS IN LANGUAGE" DEPARTMENT

English words of *Nahuatl* (Aztec) origin include "avocado," "chili," "chocolate," "coyote," and "tomato."

. . . prime examples of how English can "absorb" words from other languages and make them "English." - LCG

Thought for Today (August 6)

THE "AND HE SHOULD KNOW" DEPARTMENT

"Government is not the solution to our problem. Government is the problem." - Ronald Reagan

----

. . . only government can legislate a course of action that creates a problem that will require government action at some future date. - LCG

Thought for Today (August 7)

THE "PLAYING POKER FOR KEEPS" DEPARTMENT

Marriage is like a deck of cards. In the beginning all you need is two hearts and a diamond. By the end, you wish you had a club and a spade.

> \- Author Unknown (probably by choice)

. . . marriage makes jokers out of all of us. - LCG

Thought for Today (August 8)

THE "SNAIL GOING THROUGH MOLASSES" DEPARTMENT

You know how to slow up the aging process? Make it go through Congress.

You know how to slow up Congress? Ah . . . if you do, please do not tell anyone. - LCG

Thought for Today (August 9)

THE "POPULAR POLITICAL POLEMICS" DEPARTMENT

"In modern government politics has taken the place of mere tyranny. The result has been more killing in the past century than in all the preceding centuries combined." – P. J. O'Rourke

---

Politicians are the only people in the world who create problems and then campaign against them. - LCG

Thought for Today (August 10)

THE "ESPECIALLY ON A WORKDAY" DEPARTMENT

"Half the day I wonder if it's too late for coffee

. . . The other half I wonder if it's too early for alcohol."

- Ron Swanson

. . . just put the alcohol in the coffee — no more problem. - LCG

Thought for Today (August 11)

THE "POPULAR POLITICAL POLEMICS" DEPARTMENT

What do gorillas and politicians have in common?
Nothing. Gorillas are intelligent, noble, and have a strong
sense of ethics.

"Politics" is derived from the Greek words "poly" (meaning many) and
"ticks" (meaning blood-sucking parasites). - LCG

Thought for Today (August 12)

THE "PRESUMPTUOUS POLITICAL POLEMICS"
DEPARTMENT

"The political machine triumphs because it is a united
minority against a divided majority." - Will Durant

The political end engenders the political necessity, which
justifies the political expedient. – Lawrence C. Gambone

"Politicians and diapers must be changed often, and for
the same reason." - Mark Twain

Politicians get votes from the poor and campaign funds from the rich by
promising to protect each from the other. - LCG

Thought for Today (August 13)

THE "WHAT'S IN A WORD" DEPARTMENT

Definitions According To The "Esoteric Dictionary"

ABOMINABLE: A male cow who ingested TNT

AVOIDABLE: What a bullfighter tries to do

BALONEY: Where some hemlines fall

CLAUSTROPHOBIC: People who are afraid of Santa Claus

COUNTERFEITTERS: People who put together kitchen cabinets

FREE RADICAL: A Demonstrator who makes bail

ILLEGAL: A sick bird

LACKADAISICAL: A shortage of flowers

LAUGHING STOCK: Cattle with a sense of humor

PARADOX: Two physicians

PHARMACIST: Someone who helps on a farm

POLARIZE: What penguins use to see

RELIEF: What trees do in the spring

SUBDUED: That's like, a guy who, like, you know, works in a submarine, man

\--

Thought for Today (August 14)

THE "LET'S ACT SOCIALLY" DEPARTMENT

The Social Security Act[44] was signed by President Franklin Delano Roosevelt (FDR) on August 14, 1935, as an act to provide for the general welfare by establishing a system of Federal old-age benefits, and by enabling individual States to make more adequate provision for aged persons, blind persons, dependent and crippled children, maternal and child welfare, public health, and the administration of their unemployment.

Social Security taxes were collected for the first time in January 1937 and the first one-time, lump-sum payments were made that same month. Regular ongoing monthly benefits started in January 1940.

Although Social Security did not really arrive in America until 1935, there were some important precursors. The first national pension program for soldiers was passed in early 1776, prior to the signing of the Declaration of Independence. Following the end of the Revolutionary War, various limited pensions were paid to veterans. But it was with the creation of Civil War pensions that a full-fledged pension system developed in America for the first time.

Immediately following the Civil War, disabled persons or survivors of deceased breadwinners comprised a much

---

[44] https://en.wikipedia.org/wiki/Social_Security_Act (accessed 6/17/18)

higher proportion of America's population than at any time in America's history. This led to the development of a generous pension program, which contained later developments that influenced the progression to Social Security.

"We can never insure one hundred percent of the population against one hundred percent of the hazards and vicissitudes of life, but we have tried to frame a law which will give some measure of protection to the average citizen and to his family against the loss of a job and against poverty-ridden old age."

- President Roosevelt upon signing the Social Security Act

. . . well, I hope now you feel socially secure. - LCG

Thought for Today (August 15)

THE "DUMB BLOND JOKES" DEPARTMENT

"Dumb blonde jokes don't offend me because I know I'm not dumb . . . and I know I'm not blonde." - Dolly Parton

----

"I'm blonde; what's your excuse?" - Reese Witherspoon

Thought for Today (August 16)

THE "MEET ME AT MID-POINT" DEPARTMENT

"The average IQ in America is—and this can be proven mathematically—average." - P. J. O'Rourke

----

Most likely, half the people you know are below average. - LCG

Thought for Today (August 17)

THE "LET'S MONKEY AROUND" DEPARTMENT

MIZARU, KIKAZARU, IWAZARU

The three wise monkeys (sometimes called the three mystic apes) are a pictorial maxim. The three monkeys are *Mizaru*, covering his eyes; *Kikazaru*, covering his ears; and *Iwazaru*, covering his mouth.[45] Together they embody the proverbial principle, "see no evil, hear no evil, speak no evil."

The source that popularized this pictorial maxim is a 17th-century carving over a door of the famous Tōshō-gū shrine in Nikkō, Japan. Carved by Hidari Jingoro, there are a total of eight panels, and the iconic three monkeys picture comes from panel 2. The philosophy, however, most likely came to Japan from China in the 8th century.

In Chinese, a similar phrase exists in the *Analects of Confucius* from the 4th century BCE: "Look not at what is contrary to propriety; listen not to what is contrary to propriety; speak not what is contrary to propriety; make no movement which is contrary to propriety." It may be that this phrase was shortened and simplified after it was brought into Japan.

Though the Chinese teaching had nothing to do with monkeys (or evil), the concept of the three monkeys originated in Japanese from a simple play on words. In

---

[45] https://en.wikipedia.org/wiki/Three_wise_monkeys (accessed 6/17/18)

Japanese, the saying is, *mizaru, kikazaru, iwazaru,* "see not, hear not, speak not." The *-zaru* is a negative conjugation on the three verbs that matches *zaru*, the modified form of *saru,* meaning "monkey," when used in compounds. Thus, the saying does not include any specific reference to "evil," but can be interpreted as referring to three monkeys.

How or when the saying traveled out of Japan, or how the reference to evil became imbued, is not clear; however it is interesting to note that many cultures have similar maxims. For example, in Ethiopia there is the saying, "Let the eye fast, let the mouth fast, let the ears fast."

Think about this the next time somebody makes a monkey out of you.
- LCG

Thought for Today (August 18)

THE "IT HAPPENED TODAY" DEPARTMENT

SOME EVENTS THAT OCCURRED ON AUGUST 18:[46]

1894 - US Congress Created the Bureau of Immigration.

1909 - Mayor of Tokyo, Yukio Ozaki, presented Washington, D.C. with 2,000 cherry trees, which President Taft decided to plant near the Potomac River.

1956 - Elvis Presley's "Hound Dog" and "Don't Be Cruel" both reached #1.

1969 - Woodstock Music & Art Fair closed with Jimi Hendrix and the Band of Gypsys as the final act.

I wonder: would it be cruel if Elvis' Hound Dog "watered" Ozaki's trees?
- LCG

---

[46] https://www.onthisday.com/events/august/18 (accessed 6/17/18)

Thought for Today (August 19)

THE "BETCHA DIDN'T KNOW THIS" DEPARTMENT

Why Sunday is called . . . "Sunday"

During the 1st and 2nd century, the Roman 8-day *nundinal* cycle was replaced with a week of seven days, and the Roman names of the planets were given to each successive day.

Germanic peoples adopted the week from the Romans as a division of time, but they changed the Roman names into those of corresponding Teutonic deities. Hence, for Sunday, the Latin *dies Solis* ("day of the sun") became the German, *Sonntag*.

The English noun Sunday derived sometime before 1250 from *sunedai*, which itself developed from Old English (before 700) *Sunnandæg* (literally meaning "sun's day"), which is cognate to other Germanic languages, including Old Frisian *sunnandei*, Old Saxon *sunnundag*, Middle Dutch *sonnendach* (modern Dutch *zondag*), Old High German *sunnun tag* (modern German *Sonntag*), and Old Norse *sunnudagr* (Danish and Norwegian *søndag*, Icelandic *sunnudagur,* and Swedish *söndag*).

The unfortunate fact is that Sunday is followed by Monday. - LCG

Thought for Today (August 20)

THE "MAN-MADE" DEPARTMENT

PLUTONIUM

Plutonium, the first man-made element, was isolated from uranium on August 20, 1942, by University of Chicago scientist Glen Seaborg.[47]

Glenn Theodore Seaborg (1912–1999) was involved in identifying nine transuranium[48] elements (94 through 102) and served as chairman of the U.S. Atomic Energy Commission (AEC) from 1961 to 1971. In 1951, he shared the Nobel Prize in chemistry with the physicist Edwin M. McMillan. - LCG

---

[47] https://en.wikipedia.org/wiki/Glenn_T._Seaborg (accessed 6/17/18)

[48] The transuranium elements (also known as transuranic elements) are the chemical elements with atomic numbers greater than 92 (the atomic number of uranium). All of these elements are unstable and decay radioactively into other elements.

Thought for Today (August 21)

THE ". . . AND THEN THERE WERE FIFTY" DEPARTMENT

Hawaii, the 50th state, entered the Union on August 21, 1959. Its capital is Honolulu; and its State Motto is, "*Ua Mau ke Ea o ka Aina i ka Pono*" (The life of the land is perpetuated in righteousness).

"Bird in ma hand plenty mo bettah dan two mo bird ina bush"
- Hawaiian Proverb

"To be, or no can be. What da question?" - Hawaiian Shakespeare

Thought for Today (August 22)

THE "WORDS OF WISDOM" DEPARTMENT

"The best way to get ahead is to move your behind."

- Larry Winget

. . . And the best way to get behind is to sit on it. - LCG

Thought for Today (August 23)

THE "YOU READ IT IN TRAFFIC" DEPARTMENT

BUMPER STICKER:

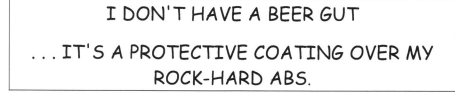
I DON'T HAVE A BEER GUT

... IT'S A PROTECTIVE COATING OVER MY ROCK-HARD ABS.

... I woke up one morning and discovered that, somehow, my flat stomach and massive chest had switched places overnight. - LCG

Thought for Today (August 24)

THE "HOME AND GARDEN" DEPARTMENT

"There is no known way to kill crabgrass that does not involve nuclear weapons." - Dave Barry

---

... I need the crabgrass; it's the only thing green in my lawn! - LCG

Thought for Today (August 25)

THE "YEAH, RIGHT!" DEPARTMENT

A few years ago, I received an email from a friend that contained a bunch of little trivia "facts." One of those facts was this:

"Five—Mozart's age when he wrote 'Twinkle, Twinkle, Little Star.'"

Since I never assume that everything you receive in an email is true (except when the email comes from me), I looked up this bit of trivia. From several different sources I discovered that the melody to "Twinkle, Twinkle, Little Star" is ubiquitous—most likely you didn't realize this, but it is used for "Baa Baa Black Sheep" and "The Alphabet Song," as well as popular Chinese and Filipino songs, and a German Christmas Carol.

The melody is derived from an old French folk song called, "*Ah! Vous dirais-je Maman*" ("Ah! Shall I tell you Mother"). About fifty years after the melody was published, it was merged with "The Star," a nursery rhyme written in 1806 by London poets Jane and Ann Taylor, and . . . well, actually . . . how and when the poem and the tune came together to form the song "Twinkle, Twinkle, Little Star" is a bit of a mystery, because the first time they're seen in print as a song is in a book published in 1838 called, *The Singing Master*.

But, how did Mozart, of all people, get credit, albeit erroneously, for writing this song?

In 1781, when he was 25 (not five), and when "*Ah! Vous dirais-je Maman*" was an old classic already, Mozart composed twelve variations of the simple tune. Unfortunately, he wasn't alone; plenty of other classical composers, including Franz Liszt and Johann Bach, had composed variations, too.

Obviously, the melody was popular with or without Mozart; and, most certainly, he didn't originate it. But, even without "Twinkle, Twinkle Little Star," Wolfgang's musical resume is pretty solid; so, I think it's ok that he didn't originate this melody.

Now, be honest: You sang "Baa Baa Black Sheep" and the "Alphabet Song" to yourself, didn't you? - LCG

Thought for Today (August 26)

THE "REALLY DEEP THOUGHTS" DEPARTMENT

"Maybe in order to understand mankind, we have to look at the word itself . . . . Basically, it's made up of two separate words - 'mank' and 'ind.' What do these words mean? It's a mystery, and that's why so is mankind."

- Jack Handey

"Mankind" spelled backwards is "Dniknam" (I don't get it either). - LCG

Thought for Today (August 27)

THE "POLITICALLY PREPOSTEROUS" DEPARTMENT

"Years ago, fairy tales began with 'Once upon a time' ... now they begin with, 'If I'm elected.'" - Carolyn Warner

------

... yeah, and they end happily never after! - LCG

Thought for Today (August 28)

THE "BOND, JAMES BOND" DEPARTMENT

"Once is chance, twice is coincidence, three times is an enemy action."- Ian Fleming

------

... four times and it becomes obvious that you are missing something that is very, very important. - LCG

Thought for Today (August 29)

THE "NOW, ISN'T THAT SPECIAL" DEPARTMENT

"Be yourself. The world worships the original."

— Ingrid Bergman

Ingrid Bergman, a Swedish actress who starred in a variety of European and American films, was born August 29, 1915. She won three Academy Awards, two Emmy Awards, four Golden Globe Awards, a BAFTA Award, and the Tony Award for Best Actress. She passed away on her 67th birthday, August 29, 1982. - LCG

Thought for Today (August 30)

THE "WORDS OF WISDOM" DEPARTMENT

"Basically, when you get to my age, you'll really measure your success in life by how many of the people you want to have love you actually do love you." - Warren Buffett

---

. . . Warren Edward Buffett (born August 30, 1930) is an American business magnate, investor, and philanthropist. At the time of this printing, he serves as the chairman/CEO of Berkshire Hathaway. - LCG

Thought for Today (August 31)

THE "TAKE A CHANCE ON THIS" DEPARTMENT

"How dare we speak of the laws of chance? Is not chance the antithesis of all law?" - Bertrand Russell

---

. . . and is not law, by chance, the antithesis of all "possibilities?" - LCG

Lawrence C. Gambone

SEPTEMBER

September

September (from Latin *septem*, "seven") was the seventh month on the oldest known Roman calendar, which had 10 months only, and in which March (Latin *martius*) held the position of the first month of the year.

In 713 BCE, King Numa Pompilius reformed the calendar by adding January and February to "nameless" winter months of the year. This moved September to the ninth month; nevertheless, it retained its name. It had 29 days until the Julian reform, in 45 BCE, which added a day to September, but kept it as the ninth month.

The Anglo-Saxons usually harvested barley in September and, thus, called the month *Gerstmonath*, barley month.

Lawrence C. Gambone

Thought for Today (September 1)

THE "WORDS OF WISDOM" DEPARTMENT

"Two things you will never be without: your reputation and your credit rating. You can destroy both in an instant and spend the rest of your life trying to get them back." - Larry Winget

----

. . . to err is human, but it takes dedication and hard work to really screw things up. - LCG

Thought for Today (September 2)

THE "BOOB TUBE" DEPARTMENT

"Television is a medium because anything well done is rare." - Fred Allen

----

Today, watching television involves violence and foul language . . . and that's just deciding who gets to hold the remote control. - LCG

Thought for Today (September 3)

THE "WORDS OF WISDUMB" DEPARTMENT

"Always predict the worst and you'll be hailed as a prophet." – Andrew Ford

----

"Write a wise saying and your name will live forever." - Anonymous

186

Thought for Today (September 4)

THE "WHY POLITICIANS ARE POLITICIANS" DEPARTMENT

"A politician looks forward to the next election. A statesman looks forward to the next generation."

- Thomas Jefferson

. . . And that's why there are no statesmen in Congress. - LCG

Thought for Today (September 5)

THE "INFINITE STUPIDITY QUOTE" DEPARTMENT

"Two things are infinite: the universe and human stupidity; and I'm not sure about the universe."

- Albert Einstein

. . . What about infinity? Isn't that infinite? - LCG

Thought for Today (September 6)

THE "WHAT'S IN A NAME" DEPARTMENT

The Marquis de La Fayette's full name:

Marie-Joseph Paul Yves Roch Gilbert du Motier de La Fayette, Marquis de Lafayette

----

. . . But his friends just called him: Marie-Joseph Paul Yves Roch Gilbert du Motier de La Fayette, Marquis de La Fayette.

The marquis was born September 6, 1757 and died May 20, 1834. - LCG

Thought for Today (September 7)

THE "QUOTABLE QUOTES" DEPARTMENT

"God limited the intelligence of man. It seems unfair that he did not also limit his stupidity."

- Konrad Adenauer

Uh, oh! My next-to-the-last brain cell just died. If my last brain cell dies, I won't be able to

. . . Chrysostomus??

Thought for Today (September 8)

THE "SAGACIOUS SAYINGS" DEPARTMENT

"Half a truth is better than no politics."
- Gilbert K. Chesterton (1874-1936)

"A good politician is quite as unthinkable as an honest burglar." - H. L. Mencken (1880-1956)

"It is terrible to contemplate how few politicians are hanged." - Gilbert K. Chesterton

"Puritanism: The gnawing fear that someone, somewhere is enjoying themselves." - H. L. Mencken

"When learned men begin to use their reason, I generally discover that they haven't got any."
- Gilbert K. Chesterton

"Democracy is the art and science of running the circus from the monkey cage." - H. L. Mencken

----

The fact that they despised politicians makes Chesterton and Mencken OK in my book (which is why they are in my book). - LCG

Thought for Today (September 9)

THE "MODERN MEETING MANIA" DEPARTMENT

ARE YOU LONELY??

**Don't like working on your own?
Hate making Decisions?**

Then Call A MEETING!!

You can . . .

**SEE people
DRAW flowcharts
FEEL important
IMPRESS your colleagues**

. . . all on COMPANY TIME!!!

MEETINGS

The practical alternative to work.

Honest to God . . . in my office, they have meetings for the purpose of planning upcoming meetings! - LCG

Thought for Today (September 10)

THE "SLEIGHT OF HAND" DEPARTMENT

"The magician and the politician . . . both have to draw our attention away from what they are really doing."

– Ben Okri

. . . . I subscribe to the concept that you cannot place the words "honest" and "politician" in the same sentence. - LCG

Thought for Today (September 11)

THE "LEARN IT FROM THE LEHRER" DEPARTMENT

"I feel that if a person has problems communicating the very least he can do is to shut up." - Tom Lehrer

---

I stayed away purposely from 9/11 quotes because the infamy of that day in 2001 angers me immensely and is, therefore, a subject about which I do not wish to communicate. - LCG

Thought for Today (September 12)

THE "GET FAMOUS QUICK" DEPARTMENT

"Martyrdom is the only way a man can become famous without ability." - George Bernard Shaw

---

I have no ability; so, I guess it's a good thing I don't want to be famous.
- LCG

Thought for Today (September 13)

THE "NFL MANIA" DEPARTMENT

"Football combines the two worst things about America: Violence punctuated by committee meetings."

- George F. Will

Most sports, such as soccer and basketball, contain "possible physical mayhem." The goal is to move a ball, which may require overpowering an opposing player. Planned or scripted plays are very basic and incorporate "instinctive" reactions—the key to these games is the physical prowess or brawn of individual players.

American football, however, incorporates "planned physical mayhem." The ultimate goal is the physical domination of opposing players in order to move the ball. This means that each play is designed strategically to achieve that dominance, incorporating "learned" responses and actions—the game requires brains as well as brawn. - LCG

Thought for Today (September 14)

THE "INTELLECTUAL INEBRIATES" DEPARTMENT

Remember: Alcohol doesn't solve any problems
. . . but, then again, neither does milk.

When I drink alcohol, everyone says I'm an alcoholic. So how come when I drink Fanta no one says I'm fantastic? - LCG

Thought for Today (September 15)

THE "BIG BOOM FROM SPACE" DEPARTMENT

Until 2010, the world's oldest and largest meteorite crater (2.1 billion years old with a diameter of 180 miles), was located in Vredefort, South Africa.

However . . .

In 2010, Scientists discovered two deep scars in the earth's crust in outback Australia that are believed to mark the remains of a meteorite crater that is 250 miles in diameter, which makes it the largest ever found.[49] Each scar is more than 120 miles in diameter; and the impact site is believed to mark the spot where a meteorite split into two, moments before it slammed into the earth.

When first discovered, the crater was thought to be the third largest crater ever found; but scientists have determined now that there are two sets of remains. Dr. Andrew Glikson, from the Australian National University, said the structures could have resulted from a single meteorite which split. The crater itself has long since disappeared, but samples from the twin scars were discovered deep beneath the ground during geothermal research drilling.

---

[49] https://www.popsci.com/worlds-largest-asteroid-impact-crater-found-australia (accessed 6/17/18)

"The two asteroids must each have been over ten kilometres [six miles] across – it would have been curtains for many life species on the planet at the time," Glikson said. "Large impacts like these may have had a far more significant role in the Earth's evolution than previously thought."

Evidence of the impact zone was found more than 1.2 miles underground in the Warburton Basin, near the borders of the states of South Australia and Queensland and the Northern Territory.

Dr. Glikson said the date of the impact was unclear but it probably occurred more than 300 million years ago.

. . . They can find craters that are 1.2 miles underground. I can't find my car keys. - LCG

Thought for Today (September 16)

THE "TELL IT LIKE IT IS" DEPARTMENT

"Why do gas stations lock their bathrooms? Are they afraid someone will clean them?" - George Carlin

. . . . does this qualify as toilet humor? - LCG

Thought for Today (September 17)

THE "YOU SHOULD KNOW THIS" DEPARTMENT

Constitution Day and Citizenship Day

The delegates to the Constitutional Convention in Philadelphia signed the Constitution of the United States of America on September 17, 1787.

Constitution Day (or Citizenship Day) is an American federal observance on this date that recognizes the adoption of the United States Constitution and those who have become U.S. citizens.

The law establishing the present holiday was created in 2004. Before this law was enacted, the holiday was known as "Citizenship Day." In addition to renaming the holiday "Constitution Day and Citizenship Day," the law mandates that all publicly funded educational institutions, and all federal agencies, provide educational programming on the history of the American Constitution on that day. In May 2005, the United States Department of Education announced the enactment of this law and that it would apply to any school receiving federal funds of any kind.

The law doesn't give American workers a day off, which is why, unfortunately, most Americans do not appreciate the historical significance of this important date.

Another good trivia question: Ask your friends to tell you the date the US Constitution was ratified. You'll be surprised at the number of people who will not know the answer. Be honest: Did you know the ratification date before you read this "Thought For Today?" - LCG

Thought for Today (September 18)

THE "STRAIGHT TO THE POINT" DEPARTMENT

"Anyway, no drug, not even alcohol, causes the fundamental ills of society. If we're looking for the source of our troubles, we shouldn't test people for drugs, we should test them for stupidity, ignorance, greed and love of power." - P. J. O'Rourke

----

. . . I agree. What I do when I'm stoned or drunk is none of my business. - LCG

Thought for Today (September 19)

THE "LEARN IT FROM THE LEHRER" DEPARTMENT

"When I was in college, there were certain words you couldn't say in front of a girl. Now you can say them, but you can't say 'girl.'" - Tom Lehrer

----

You go, gir . . . ah . . . person of non-male gender! - LCG

Thought for Today (September 20)

THE "EMPIRICAL RESULTS" DEPARTMENT

In a recent survey, 90% of the men interviewed said a woman's eyes were the first thing they noticed. In that same survey, 100% of the women interviewed said that men are liars.

. . . uh . . . the "eyes" have it. - LCG

Thought for Today (September 21)

THE "WRIGHT IS NEVER WRONG" DEPARTMENT

"Support Bacteria . . . They're the only culture some people have." - Steven Wright

---
If we want culture, we have to stop making stupid people famous. - LCG

Thought for Today (September 22)

THE "IT HAPPENED YEARS AGO TODAY" DEPARTMENT

EVENTS THAT OCCURRED ON SEPTEMBER 22:[50]

1515 - Anne of Cleeves, fourth wife of Henry the VIII, was born in Cleeves, Germany.

1692 - The last person was hanged for witchcraft in Salem, Massachusetts.

1711 - The Tuscarora Indian War began with a massacre of settlers in North Carolina.

1735 - Robert Walpole became the 1st British PM to live at 10 Downing Street.

1776 - With no trial, American Captain Nathan Hale was hanged as a spy by the British in New York City.

1789 - Congress authorized the office of Postmaster-General.

1893 - Charles and Frank Duryea showed off the first American automobile produced for sale to the public.

1914 - A German submarine sank 3 British ironclads, alerting the British to the effectiveness of the submarine: 1,459 died.

---

[50] https://www.onthisday.com/events/september/22 (accessed 6/17/18)

1920 - Chicago grand jury convened to investigate charges that 8 White Sox players conspired to fix the 1919 World Series.

1939 - Junko Tabei, the 1st woman to climb Mount Everest, was born in Japan.

1945 - President Truman accepted U.S. Secretary of War Stimson's recommendation to designate the war "World War II."

1948 - Lawrence C. Gambone was born to Italian immigrant parents in Camden, New Jersey.

1955 - Commercial TV began in England. ITV began broadcasting at 7:15 pm in the London region only.

1958 - The nuclear submarine USS Skate remained a record 31 days under the North Pole.

1959 - The first telephone cable linking Europe and the United States was inaugurated.

1961 - President John Kennedy signed a congressional act establishing the Peace Corps.

1969 - Willie Mays of the San Francisco Giants became the first baseball player since Babe Ruth to hit 600 home runs.

1970 - President Richard M. Nixon signed a bill giving the District of Columbia representation in the U.S. Congress.

1973 - Dallas-Fort Worth International Airport was dedicated. It was constructed to accommodate the new jumbo jets.

1975 - Sara Jane Moore, an FBI informer and self-proclaimed revolutionary, attempted to shoot President Gerald Ford.

1980 - Iraq under Saddam Hussein invaded Iran following border skirmishes and a dispute over the Shatt al-Arab waterway.

2003 - The jawbone of a man, found in 2002 in Romania, was reported as the oldest fossil from an early modern human to be found in Europe. It was carbon-dated to between 34,000 and 36,000 years ago.

September 22 . . . it was a very good day/year. - LCG

Thought for Today (September 23)

THE "WORDS OF WISDOM" DEPARTMENT

"Learn from the mistakes of others. You can never live long enough to make them all yourself." - Groucho Marx

---

. . . Yeah, but I'm cramming in as many as I can while I can. - LCG

Thought for Today (September 24)

THE "I MAY BE MISTAKEN, BUT...." DEPARTMENT

"A computer lets you make more mistakes faster than any invention in human history—with the possible exceptions of handguns and tequila." – Mitch Ratcliffe

----

. . . did somebody say "tequila?" - LCG

Thought for Today (September 25)

THE "SIR WINSTON'S WISDOM" DEPARTMENT

"The inherent vice of capitalism is the unequal sharing of blessings. The inherent virtue of Socialism is the equal sharing of miseries."

– Winston Churchill

Sir Winston Leonard Spencer-Churchill KG OM CH TD PCc DL FRS RA (November 30, 1874 - January 24, 1965) was a British statesman, army officer, and writer, who served as Prime Minister of the United Kingdom from 1940 to 1945 and again from 1951 to 1955. - LCG

Thought for Today (September 26)

THE "SYFY SURVIVAL TIPS" DEPARTMENT

It has become a science fiction movie cliché: Young actors and actresses in critical situations fail to reach the final credits because they make some really dumb moves. Therefore, as a service to science fiction cast members everywhere, here is a set of 10 "SYFY Survival Tips" that they (and the general public also) should follow:

1. Never, ever go first.
2. If the birds take off, and the animals dart away, run! Fast!
3. If the door is steel-plated and triple-barred, don't open it.
4. If the entrance is dark and you hear inexplicable sounds, for crying out loud, don't go in.
5. If you have a book that can summon the dead, don't read it out loud.
6. If you find yourself alone in a dark, sinister-looking room, refrain from calling, "Hello! Is anybody in here?"
7. If he starts growing fur, he is no longer your boyfriend.
8. If you come upon a strange, glowing, pulsating object, don't reach out to touch it.
9. Never, ever be last.
10. Never moon a werewolf.

. . . better still, try acting in a nice, safe romantic comedy. - LCG

Thought for Today (September 27)

THE "CLASSICAL POLITICAL QUOTECALS" DEPARTMENT

"Human nature is evil, and goodness is caused by intentional activity." - Xun Zi (310-238 BCE)

"Avarice has seized mankind that wealth possesses them rather than they possess wealth."
- Pliny the Elder (23-79 CE)

"A penalty for refusing to participate in politics is that you end up being governed by your inferiors."
- Plato (429-347 BCE)

"Because you don't take an interest in politics doesn't mean politics won't take an interest in you."
- Pericles (430 BCE)

"A tyrant is always stirring up some war or other, in order that the people may require a leader."
- Plato (429-347 BCE)

"He who has lost honor can lose nothing more."
- Publilius Syrus (46 BCE)

"Manifest plainness, Embrace simplicity, Reduce selfishness, Have few desires." - Lao Tzu (500 BCE)

Thought for Today (September 28)

THE "MOST MEMORABLY NON-QUOTED" DEPARTMENT

"If you aren't liberal when you are young, you have no heart. If you aren't conservative when you are old, you have no brain." - (attributed to Winston Churchill)

This grand sentiment ranked as my favorite Winston Churchill quote . . . until I found out that there is no record of anyone having heard Churchill say it. Paul Addison of Edinburgh University made this comment: "Surely Churchill can't have used the words attributed to him. He'd been a Conservative at 15 and a Liberal at 35!" - LCG

Thought for Today (September 29)

THE "YOU READ IT ON THE ROAD" DEPARTMENT

BUMPER STICKERS:

ORGANIZED LOCAL DISTRAUGHT FATHERS AGAINST REBELLIOUS TEENAGERS (OLDFART)

BODY BY BOWFLEX . . . BRAIN BY MATTEL!

DON'T STEAL FROM PEOPLE . . . THE GOVERNMENT HATES COMPETITION!

BUMPER STICKER: My Life is Based on a True Story. - LCG

Thought for Today (September 30)

THE "LET'S IRON THIS OUT" DEPARTMENT

In mid-2016, scientists wrapped up a mystery that had been puzzling archaeologists since Howard Carter found King Tutankhamen's tomb in 1922. Among the items buried with the young pharaoh was a dagger made of iron.[51] This was unusual; ironwork in Egypt 3,300 years ago was incredibly rare; and the dagger had not rusted.

An examination with an X-ray fluorescence spectrometer revealed that the metal used for the dagger was of extraterrestrial origin . . . . No, not "little green men;" the high levels of cobalt and nickel matched that of known meteorites recovered from the Red Sea.

Because several ancient Egyptian texts referenced "iron of the sky," archaeologists had long suspected that Egyptian iron objects were made from meteorites and, in 2013, they tested an ancient iron artifact. It had been made using meteorite fragments. This result led to the eventual testing of Tutankhamen's dagger.

There were several items recovered from the pharaoh's tomb that were made of iron; archeologists now believe they, too, were crafted using meteorite iron.

. . . Personally, I was hoping it was "little green men." - LCG

---

[51] https://en.wikipedia.org/wiki/Tutankhamun%27s_meteoric_iron_dagger (accessed 6/17/18)

Lawrence C. Gambone

OCTOBER

October

Originally the eighth month in the old Roman 10-month calendar (from the Latin *ôctō* meaning "eight"), October became the tenth month, but retained its name, after January and February were inserted into the calendar around 713 BCE.

Commonly, October is associated with the season of autumn in the Northern hemisphere and with spring in the Southern hemisphere.

Thought for Today (October 1)

THE "EXTRA EFFORT" DEPARTMENT

I always give 100% at work:

12% Monday;

23% Tuesday;

40% Wednesday;

20% Thursday;

5% Friday.

Actually, it's a wash: I don't do much work; they don't give me much pay. - LCG

Thought for Today (October 2)

THE "CELEBRITY BIRTHDAY" DEPARTMENT

Groucho Marx

"*Whatever it is, I'm against it.*" - Groucho Marx

Born Julius Henry Marx on October 2, 1890, in New York, Groucho was an American comedian and film star. He made 26 feature films, 13 of them with his siblings, the Marx Brothers, of whom he was the third-born. In addition, he had a successful solo career, most notably as the host of the radio and television game show *You Bet Your Life*.

"*Who are you going to believe, me or your own eyes?*"
- Groucho Marx

His distinctive appearance, carried over from his days in vaudeville, included quirks such as an exaggerated stooped posture, glasses, cigar, and a thick greasepaint mustache and eyebrows. These exaggerated features resulted in the creation of one of the world's most ubiquitous and recognizable novelty disguises, known as "Groucho Glasses": a one-piece mask consisting of horn-rimmed glasses, large plastic nose, bushy eyebrows, and mustache.

"*Those are my principles. If you don't like them, I have others.*" - Groucho Marx

After a few stabs at entry-level office work and jobs suitable for adolescents, Julius took to the stage as a boy singer in 1905. Marx claimed that he was "hopelessly average" as a vaudevillian. He was joined by his brothers later to form what Wikipedia cites as "a forgettable-quality vaudeville singing group billed as 'The Four Nightingales'." After a rather dispirited performance in Nacogdoches, Texas, the boys began cracking jokes on stage, which, to their surprise, was better received by the audience than their singing.

"One man in 1000 is a leader of men . . . The other 999 follow women." - Groucho Marx

The Marx Brothers' first movies were recreations of their successful Broadway plays. Their first movie was a silent film made in 1921 that was never released and was lost or destroyed subsequently. The next two films, *The Cocoanuts* (1929) and *Animal Crackers* (1930) were filmed on Long Island, New York. The rest were filmed in Hollywood.

"Say the magic word and win a hundred dollars."
– Groucho Marx

In 1947 Marx was chosen to host a radio quiz program, *You Bet Your Life*, broadcast by ABC. It moved to CBS for a brief period, before moving over to NBC radio and television in 1950. Filmed before a live audience, the television show consisted of Marx interviewing contestants and adlibbing jokes, before playing a brief quiz. The television show ran for 11 successful seasons until it was canceled in 1961.

"No man goes before his time . . . unless the boss leaves early." - Groucho Marx

Groucho Marx was hospitalized at Cedars Sinai Medical Center with pneumonia on June 22, 1977, and died at the age of 86 on August 19, 1977. His death was overshadowed somewhat by the death of Elvis Presley, three days earlier. In an interview, he jokingly suggested his epitaph: "Excuse me, I can't stand up."

"The world would not be in such a snarl, had Marx been Groucho instead of Karl." - Irving Berlin

Thought for Today (October 3)

THE "PUPPY LOVE" DEPARTMENT

"There is no psychiatrist in the world like a puppy licking your face." - Bernard Williams

"A dog is the only thing on earth that loves you more the he loves himself." - Josh Billings

"The average dog is a nicer person than the average person." - Andrew A. Rooney

----

I can say honestly that my wife doesn't treat me like a dog . . . . She treats our dog much better than me. - LCG

Thought for Today (October 4)

THE "DOG DOGMA" DEPARTMENT

Created by Charles M. Schulz, Snoopy, the Peanuts comic strip's best-known character, first appeared on October 4, 1950. Since his debut, Snoopy has become one of the most recognizable and iconic characters in the comic strip.

. . . The original drawings of Snoopy were inspired by Spike, one of Charles M. Schulz's childhood dogs. - LCG

Thought for Today (October 5)

THE "LEARN IT FROM THE LEHRER" DEPARTMENT

"I know that there are people who do not love their fellow man, and I HATE people like that!" - Tom Lehrer

------

"If you can't be with the one you love, honey, love the one you're with."
- Stephen Stills

Thought for Today (October 6)

THE "NON-FAMOUS SIBLINGS" DEPARTMENT

We Seldom Consider The Fact That Famous (And Infamous) People Had Not-So-Famous Siblings:

Bleda the Hun — Elder brother of Attila

Paula Hitler — Younger sister of Adolf

Maria Ulyanova — Younger sister of Lenin

Caspar van Beethoven — Unmusical brother of Ludwig

Gebhard Himmler — Elder brother of Heinrich

Henrietta Marx — Younger sister of Karl

Feodor the not even remotely Terrible — Younger brother of Ivan

Pierre d'Arc — Younger brother of Joan

Mao Zemin — Little brother of Mao Tse Tung

Billy — The drunk and dumber brother of President Jimmy Carter

Ronald — The, smarter, better looking, more successful brother of Lawrence Gambone

---

. . . for advice, I talk to my brother; for expert advice, I talk to myself.
- LCG

Thought for Today (October 7)

THE "IT HAPPENED YEARS AGO TODAY" DEPARTMENT

On October 7, 1916, Georgia Tech. beat Cumberland College 222 to 0 — the worst football defeat in football history.[52]

Cumberland College, a Presbyterian school in Lebanon, Tennessee, had discontinued its football program before the season but was not allowed to cancel its game against the Georgia Tech Engineers. Georgia Tech coach John Heisman insisted on the schools' scheduling agreement, which required Cumberland to pay $3,000 ($75,000 in inflation-adjusted terms) to Tech if its football team failed to show. To ensure the game was played, Heisman offered Cumberland $500 to cover the cost of transportation to Atlanta.

So, Cumberland's "baseball" team student manager put together a team of 16 players, most of whom were his fraternity brothers, to travel to Atlanta as Cumberland's football team. The game was played on October 7, 1916.

The Engineers led 63–0 after the first quarter and 126–0 at halftime. Tech added 54 more points in the third quarter and 42 in the final period. Cumberland was intercepted 6 times, and fumbled 9 times, losing the ball each time. Cumberland's greatest pass play was a ten-yard pass (that came on 4th and 22); its greatest running

---

[52] https://en.wikipedia.org/wiki/1916_Cumberland_vs._Georgia_Tech_football _game (accessed 6/17/18)

play occurred when its fullback ran around the right end for a loss of 6 yards. Cumberland's most effective play was a blocked extra-point.

STATISTICS

Team	Rushing				Passing				Kicking	
	Att	Yards	TD	Fumb Lost	Comp–Att	Yards	TD	Int	FGM–FGA	XPM–XPA
Cumberland	27	−42	0	9	2–18	14	0	6	0–0	0–0
Georgia Tech	40	978	32	0	0–0	0	0	0	0–0	30–32

RECORDS

Since World War II, only a handful of schools have topped 100 points in a college football game. The modern-era record for most points scored is 106, set by Fort Valley State (Georgia) against Knoxville College in 1969. In 1968, Houston defeated Tulsa 100–6 to set the NCAA record in major college football. In 1949 the University of Wyoming defeated the University of Northern Colorado 103-0. The Division III football scoring record was set in 1968 when North Park University defeated North Central College 104-32, with ten passing touchdowns.

NOTE: John Heisman, Georgia Tech's coach, was inducted into the College Football Hall of Fame as a coach in 1954. The Heisman Trophy, awarded annually to the season's most outstanding college football player, is named after him. - LCG

Thought for Today (October 8)

THE "REALITY BITES" DEPARTMENT

So, you think you have influence?
Try ordering someone else's dog around.

. . . Try to be the person your dog thinks you are. - LCG

Thought for Today (October 9)

THE "LET'S PUT IT IN PERSPECTIVE" DEPARTMENT

"Let's say you're going to a party, so you pull out some pocket change and buy a little greeting card that plays 'Happy Birthday' when it's opened. After the party, someone casually tosses the card into the trash, throwing away more computer power than existed in the entire world before 1950." - John Huey

---

Hey! The ingrate just casually tossed away your birthday card! - LCG

Thought for Today (October 10)

THE "WORDS ON LIFE" DEPARTMENT

"Life is essentially a cheat and its conditions are those of defeat; the redeeming things are not happiness and pleasure but the deeper satisfactions that come out of struggle." - F. Scott Fitzgerald

---

Uh . . . I'm inspired . . . I think . . . maybe . . . . What about you? - LCG

Thought for Today (October 11)

THE "DISPROPORTIONATE DYSFUNCTION" DEPARTMENT

Recent studies have determined that one-fourth of the population is mentally unstable. You should check your three best friends.

. . . If they're ok, then it's probably you.

. . . statistically speaking . . . . - LCG

Thought for Today (October 12)

THE "SIR WINSTON'S WISDOM" DEPARTMENT

"Many forms of Government have been tried, and will be tried in this world of sin and woe. No one pretends that democracy is perfect or all-wise. Indeed it has been said that democracy is the worst form of Government except for all those other forms that have been tried from time to time . . . ."

– Winston Churchill

. . . this quote is genuine. It was made by Sir Winston on November 11, 1947. - LCG

Thought for Today (October 13)

THE "U. S. MILITARY HISTORY" DEPARTMENT

Birth of the United States Navy . . .

On 13 October 1775, the Second Continental Congress passed a resolution creating the Continental Navy. Although the United States Navy was disbanded, reinstated, revamped, and reorganized on several occasions, this is recognized as its official birthdate.

"I joined the Navy to see the world. But, what do I see? I see the sea."
- Bugs Bunny

Thought for Today (October 14)

THE "PONDERING PERSPECTIVES" DEPARTMENT

"Some see the glass as half-empty, some see the glass as half-full. I see the glass as too big." - George Carlin

---

If you used a mug instead of a glass, would you have this problem?
- LCG

Thought for Today (October 15)

THE "TIME FOR LUNCH" DEPARTMENT

"Time's fun when you're having flies." - Kermit the Frog

Time may be a great healer . . . . But it's a lousy beautician. - LCG

Thought for Today (October 16)

THE "HINTS FOR THE STRAIGHT SHOOTER" DEPARTMENT

To ensure you always hit the target, shoot first

. . . then call whatever you hit the target.

. . . just be sure that whatever you hit is not alive or expensive. - LCG

Thought for Today (October 17)

THE "LEARN IT FROM THE LEHRER" DEPARTMENT

"It is sobering to consider that when Mozart was my age he had already been dead for two years." - Tom Lehrer

---

. . . But the boy could play. - LCG

Thought for Today (October 18)

THE "IF YOU SAY SO" DEPARTMENT

"An expert is a person who has made all the mistakes that can be made in a very narrow field."
 - Niels Bohr (Nobel Prize winner)

According to Mr. Bohr's definition, I'm an expert in everything! - LCG

Thought for Today (October 19)

THE "NOW, THAT MAKES SENSE" DEPARTMENT

"Never argue with stupid people, they will drag you down to their level and then beat you with experience."
 - Mark Twain

. . . and . . . is that why I never win an argument with my wife? - LCG

Thought for Today (October 20)

THE "INCONSEQUENTIAL QUOTES" DEPARTMENT

"We are all a little weird and life's a little weird, and when we find someone whose weirdness is compatible with ours, we join up with them and fall in mutual weirdness and call it love." - Dr. Seuss

---

"Always remember that you are absolutely unique, just like everyone else." - Margaret Mead

Thought for Today (October 21)

THE "CLASSICAL QUOTES" DEPARTMENT

"Pay attention to your enemies, for they are the first to discover your mistakes." - Antisthenes

---

Born 445 BCE, Antisthenes was an Athenian philosopher and disciple of Socrates. He was present at Socrates' death and never forgave his master's persecutors—it is said that he was instrumental in procuring their punishment. - LCG

Thought for Today (October 22)

THE "STATIC STATISTICS" DEPARTMENT

A recent survey determined that three out of every four people make up 75% of the world's population.

Five out of every four people do not understand statistics. - LCG

Thought for Today (October 23)

THE "SIGN OF THE TIMES" DEPARTMENT

SIGN SEEN AT A RADIATOR REPAIR SHOP:

> ## THIS IS THE BEST PLACE TO TAKE A LEAK.

. . . and with that, I'll sign off for today. - LCG

Thought for Today (October 24)

THE "WORDS TO PONDER" DEPARTMENT

"Surround yourself with the dreamers and the doers, the believers and the thinkers, but most of all, surround yourself with those who see the greatness within you, even when you don't see it yourself." - Edmund Lee

----

"The key is to keep company only with people who uplift you, whose presence calls forth your best." - Epictetus (55-135 CE)

Thought for Today (October 25)

THE "ENGLISH WORDS THAT DON'T SOUND LIKE ENGLISH WORDS" DEPARTMENT

The spelling and meaning of the word *"brouhaha"* came to English directly from French in the late 19th century. The French derivation came from the Hebrew phrase *bārŪkh habbā',* meaning "blessed is he who enters." French worshippers, whose knowledge of Hebrew was limited, distorted the phrase to the word *brouhaha.* In English, the word first meant "a noisy confusion of sound," a sense that was extended later to its current reference to any tumultuous and confused situation.[53]

. . . yep, I get noisy and confused after I drink a brew, ha, ha! - LCG

Thought for Today (October 26)

THE "THIS IS PART OF US ALL" DEPARTMENT

There are 10 human body parts that are only 3 letters long: Arm, Ear, Eye, Gum, Hip, Jaw, Leg, Lip, Rib, Toe.

Until 1788, bodysnatching was not a criminal offence; however, suspects were prosecuted for theft of the coffin. - LCG

---

[53] Brouhaha was used rarely throughout the 19th and most of the 20th centuries; it is gaining popularity as a trendy expression in the 21st century.

Thought for Today (October 27)

THE "STATEMENTS FROM A STATESMAN" DEPARTMENT

"It is not the critic who counts, not the man who points out how the strong man stumbled, or where the doer of deeds could have done better. The credit belongs to the man who is actually in the arena; whose face is marred by the dust and sweat and blood; who strives valiantly; who errs and comes short again and again; who knows the great enthusiasms, the great devotions and spends himself in a worthy cause; who at the best, knows in the end the triumph of high achievement, and who, at worst, if he fails, at least fails while daring greatly; so that his place shall never be with those cold and timid souls who know neither victory or defeat."

- Theodore Roosevelt

Theodore Roosevelt Jr. (October 27, 1858 – January 6, 1919) was an American statesman and writer who served as the 26th President of the United States from 1901 to 1909. He also served as the 25th Vice President of the United States from March to September 1901 and as the 33rd Governor of New York from 1899 to 1900. As a leader of the Republican Party during this time, he became a driving force for the early 20th century's Progressive Era in the United States. His face is depicted on Mount Rushmore, alongside those of George Washington, Thomas Jefferson, and Abraham Lincoln. - LCG

Thought for Today (October 28)

THE "THERE'S ALWAYS SOMETHING" DEPARTMENT

There's always:

. . . a little truth behind every "Just Kidding"

. . . a little curiosity behind every "Just Wondering"

. . . a little knowledge behind every "I Don't Know"

. . . and a little emotion behind every "I Don't Care."

. . . and there's always a little sarcasm behind every "Wow, That Was Awesome." - LCG

Thought for Today (October 29)

THE "STUFF YOU NEVER THOUGHT ABOUT" DEPARTMENT

Why is Thursday named . . . you know, Thursday?

Thursday is named after the Norse god Thor. In the Norse languages this day is called *Torsdag*.

The Romans named Thursday, *dies Jovis* (Jove's Day), after their most important god, Jove or Jupiter. The god Woden (now called Odin) was the Norse counterpart to the Roman Jove; but Woden had a day named after him already, Wednesday (Woden's day). Therefore, it was Thor who, from among the Norse and early English gods, replaced the Roman god Jove (*dies Jovis*) as the name for the fifth day of the week.

In Norse mythology, Thor was the most popular of all the gods. He was the son of Odin (or Woden) and Frigg, and was represented as a man of middle age with red hair and beard, and he possessed enormous strength. Thor's chariot was drawn by he-goats; it was the rolling of this chariot that caused thunder. Armed with *Mjolnir* (the smasher), a terrible magic hammer, Thor aided and guarded man against evil spirits and disease. He was looked upon, especially, as the god of agriculture and was worshiped most widely for that reason.

In Middle English, Thor's name was seen sometimes as Thur and sometimes as Thunor. As a result, in Middle English, we see *Thursdæg*, *Thunresdæg*, and sometimes *Thuresday*.

Thursdæg and *Thuresday*, were the names that survived, giving us, eventually, the modern English, Thursday.

. . . Personally, I prefer to think of Thursday as "Friday-Eve." - LCG

Thought for Today (October 30)

THE "ONCE A PUN A TIME" DEPARTMENT

I'm reading a book about anti-gravity. I can't put it down.

I know a guy who's addicted to brake fluid . . . he says he can stop any time.

Velcro — what a rip off.

A vulture carrying two dead raccoons was prevented from boarding a plane because only one carrion was allowed per passenger.

Two silk worms began to race . . . . They ended up in a tie.

What do you get when you cross a snowman with a vampire? Frostbite!

I sent ten different puns to friends, hoping that at least one of the puns would get a laugh. No pun in ten did. - LCG

Thought for Today (October 31)

THE "TRICK-OR-TREAT" DEPARTMENT

A Brief History of Halloween

Today's Halloween customs have their roots in the pagan folk customs and beliefs of Celtic-speaking countries.[54] Historian Nicholas Rogers noted that while . . .

> . . . some folklorists have detected its origins in the Roman feast of Pomona, the goddess of fruits and seeds, or in the festival of the dead called Parentalia, today's Halloween is more typically linked to the Celtic festival of Samhain.

Pronounced SAH-win or SOW-in, Samhain in Celtic, means "summer's end."

Samhain included "mumming" and "guising" as far back as the 16th century in Ireland, Scotland, Wales, and the Isle of Man. Mumming and guising involved people going house-to-house in costume (or in disguise), usually reciting verses or songs in exchange for food. The first reference to "guising," or ritual begging, on Halloween occurred in North America in 1911. Another reference appeared in 1915, with a third in Chicago in 1920.

It was the Christian celebration of All Hallows' Evening that gave Halloween its name. According to Wikipedia, Halloween is the evening before the Christian holy days of All Hallows' Day (also known as All Saints' Day or Hallowmas) on 1 November, and All Souls' Day on 2

[54] https://en.wikipedia.org/wiki/Halloween (accessed 6/17/18)

November. As a result, the full name of the holiday on 31 October became All Hallows' Evening (meaning the evening before All Hallows' Day), which was shortened to All Hallows' Eve. Hallowe'en is a contraction of All Hallows' Eve, which became, finally, Halloween.

It is interesting to note that American almanacs of the late 18th and early 19th century give no indication that Halloween was celebrated widely. It was not until mass Irish and Scottish immigration in the 19th century that Halloween became a major holiday in America.

American historian and author Ruth Edna Kelley wrote in 1919, "All Halloween customs in the United States are borrowed directly or adapted from those of other countries."

Finally, trick-or-treating does not seem to have become a widespread practice in the United States until the 1930s. The earliest known use of the term "trick or treat" in print appeared in 1927 in Alberta, Canada. The first appearance of the term "trick-or-treat" in the United States occurred in 1934; however, the first use in a national publication did not occur until 1939.

What did the skeleton say when he sat down to dinner? Bone appetite!

What does a witch use for a garage? A broom closet.

Why don't skeletons go to scary movies? They don't have the guts.

Why do witches stay in the dark? Because they don't know which witch should switch which switch.

Lawrence C. Gambone

NOVEMBER

November

November is the eleventh and penultimate month of the year in both the Julian and Gregorian Calendars, the fourth and last of four months to have a length of 30 days, and the fifth and last of five months to have a length of less than 31 days.

November was the ninth month of the ancient Roman calendar (from the Latin *novem* meaning "nine"); however, it retained its name when January and February were added to the calendar and it moved to the eleventh spot.

November is a month of late spring in the Southern Hemisphere and late autumn in the Northern Hemisphere.

Thought for Today (November 1)

THE "HEADLINES WE'D LOVE TO SEE" DEPARTMENT

CONGRESS DISBANDS; MEMBERS DECIDE
THEY SHOULD WORK FOR A LIVING

ENERGIZER BUNNY ARRESTED;
CHARGED WITH BATTERY

GLOBAL WARMING PROTEST
POSTPONED DUE TO SNOW

HOLE FOUND IN NUDIST COLONY FENCE;
POLICE ARE LOOKING INTO IT

MAN LOSES 180 LBS OF UGLY FAT;
SAYS HE'S GLAD SHE LEFT

TONTO SHOT; LONE RANGER LEARNS
TRUE MEANING OF "KEMOSABE"

POLICE STATION TOILET STOLEN;
POLICE HAVE NOTHING TO GO ON

GAMBONE WINS PULITZER PRIZE (It's a headline I'd like to see). - LCG

Thought for Today (November 2)

THE "STATES OF THE UNION" DEPARTMENT[55]

NORTH DAKOTA: The 39th state entered the Union November 2, 1889. Capital: Bismarck; Motto: "Liberty and union, now and forever, one and inseparable."

SOUTH DAKOTA: The 40th state entered the Union November 2, 1889. Capital: Pierre; Motto: "Under God the people rule."

This is the only instance where two states were admitted to the Union on the same day. - LCG

Thought for Today (November 3)

THE "WALKED INTO A BAR JOKE" DEPARTMENT

The past, the present, and the future walked into a bar.

. . . It was tense.

You can groan . . . . I did. – LCG

---

[55] https://www.onthisday.com/events/november/2 (accessed 6/17/18)

Thought for Today (November 4)

THE "I KNOW THIS FROM EXPERIENCE" DEPARTMENT

"Experience: That marvelous thing that enables you to recognize a mistake when you make it again."
- Franklin Jones

Youth is that time of life when you survived experiences that most likely would kill you now.
- L. C. Gambone

"Experience is what you get when you don't get what you want."
- Tori Filler

"Character is determined more by the lack of certain experiences than by those one has had."
- Friedrich Nietzsche

Experience is something you don't get until just after you need it. - LCG

Thought for Today (November 5)

THE "IMPORTANT HOLIDAYS" DEPARTMENT

While searching for a quote to place in this slot, a thought occurred to me. November has two important holidays, which (in my opinion), though not intended, are intertwined. These holidays are Veterans' Day and Thanksgiving.

Why do I say they are intertwined? Simply because we should give thanks for the sacrifices made by our veterans.

- Lawrence C. Gambone

I am a veteran. I am proud to say that I served my country. - LCG

Thought for Today (November 6)

THE "WORDS OF WISDOM" DEPARTMENT

"When someone is going through a storm, your silent presence is more powerful than a million empty words."

- Thema Davis

In a time of need, nothing is more reassuring or inspirational than the support of one friend by another. - LCG

Thought for Today (November 7)

THE "THOUGHTS TO PONDER" DEPARTMENT

"We tend to forget that happiness doesn't come as a result of getting something we don't have, but rather of recognizing and appreciating what we do have."

- Frederick Koenig

I don't know, Fred; I recognize the fact that I don't have any money; and I'd be very happy if someone gave me a million dollars. - LCG

Thought for Today (November 8)

THE "WORDS TO WONDER ABOUT" DEPARTMENT

"If a cluttered desk is a sign of a cluttered mind, of what, then, is an empty desk a sign?" - Albert Einstein

---

. . . I believe that people who keep their desks neat are just too lazy to look for things. This guy talks like Yoda. – LCG

Thought for Today (November 9)

THE "NOW THAT YOU MENTION IT" DEPARTMENT

Why is Monday so far from Friday?

And why is Friday so close to Monday?

I know how to fix this: Rename Monday, Friday; and Friday, Monday.
- LCG

Thought for Today (November 10)

THE "STUFF YOU NEVER THOUGHT ABOUT" DEPARTMENT

Why Tuesday is . . . Well, You Know, Tuesday

According to international standard ISO 8601, Tuesday is the second day of the week. According to some commonly used calendars, however, especially in the United States, it is the third day of the week.

The English name is derived from Old English *Tiwesdæg* and Middle English *Tewesday*, meaning "Tīw's Day," the day of Tiw or Týr, who, in Norse mythology, was the god of single combat, victory, and heroic glory. Tiw was equated with Mars in the *interpretatio germanica*,[56] and the name of the day is a translation of Latin *dies Martis*.

Tuesday is associated with the planet Mars and shares that planet's symbol, ♂. Mars rules over Aries and Scorpio, therefore, these signs are associated with Tuesday also.

---

[56] *Interpretatio germanica* is the practice by the Germanic peoples of identifying Roman gods with the names of Germanic deities. This occurred around the 1st century CE, when both cultures came into closer contact.

Thought for Today (November 11)

THE "THEY SERVED OUR COUNTRY" DEPARTMENT

VETERANS DAY – November 11

World War I — known at the time as "The Great War," ended officially when the Treaty of Versailles was signed on June 28, 1919; however, a temporary cessation of hostilities had gone into effect on the eleventh hour of the eleventh day of the eleventh month of 1918. It is for that reason, November 11, 1918, is generally regarded as the end of "the war to end all wars."

An Act (52 Stat. 351; 5 US Code, Sec. 87a) approved by Congress on May 13, 1938, made the 11th of November a legal holiday. Designated "Armistice Day," it was a day set aside to honor veterans of World War I and dedicated to the cause of world peace.

In 1954, after World War II and the Korean War required the greatest mobilization of soldiers, sailors, Marines, and airmen in the Nation's history, the 83rd Congress amended the Act of 1938 by striking out the word "Armistice" and inserting in its place the word "Veterans." With the approval of this legislation (Public Law 380) on June 1, 1954, November 11th became a day to honor American veterans of all wars.[57]

SAY "THANK YOU" TO ALL VETERANS! - LCG

---

[57] https://en.wikipedia.org/wiki/Veterans_Day (accessed 6/17/18)

Thought for Today (November 12)

THE "GOOD GOD IT'S GOVERNMENT" DEPARTMENT

When purging files, a true bureaucrat will photocopy each document before discarding it.

Unfortunately, government's idea of "thinking out of the box" is simply to get a bigger box. - LCG

Thought for Today (November 13)

THE "WHO KNOWS THE REASON" DEPARTMENT

Why are there artificial ingredients in lemon juice, but real lemons in dishwashing liquid?

. . . and why does dishwashing liquid taste so bad? - LCG

Thought for Today (November 14)

THE "WHAT GOES DOWN SHOULD COME UP" DEPARTMENT

YO-YO

The yo-yo originated most likely in China and spread around the world. It is considered to be the world's second oldest toy (the doll is the oldest). [58]

A Greek vase painting from 500 BCE shows a boy playing with a yo-yo. Greek records from the period describe toys made out of wood, metal, or painted terra cotta (fired clay). The terra cotta disks were used to ceremonially offer the toys of youth to certain gods when a child came of age—discs of other materials were used for actual play.

The yo-yo was used as a hunting weapon in 16th Century Philippines. Webster's Collegiate Dictionary states that the word "yo-yo" likely derives from the northern Philippine Ilocano language word "*yóyo*".

"I tell ya when I was a kid, all I knew was rejection. My yo-yo, it never came back." - Rodney Dangerfield

---

[58] https://en.wikipedia.org/wiki/Yo-yo (accessed 6/17/18)

Thought for Today (November 15)

THE "BETCHA DIDN'T KNOW BETCHA DIDN'T CARE" DEPARTMENT

THE PANAMA CANAL

The Pacific entrance to the Panama Canal is farther east than the Atlantic entrance (check a map). [59]

Not commonly known is the fact that the two oceans have different sea levels, and different levels of high tide. At the Pacific entrance to the Panama Canal, the ocean can rise as much as 20 feet (6.07 meters), but 45 miles away, the difference between high tide and low in the Atlantic is just three feet (0.91 meters).

The average transit time through the canal is eight to ten hours.

Cost depends on a vessel's size and weight. A private yacht may pay $2,000 or less to Cross the Expanded Panama Canal;   a Containership may pay nearly $1 Million. At the time of this printing, the average cost per vessel is approximately $829,000, which is less than it would cost to sail around South America.

Interesting fact: At one time, Panama Canal authorities charged swimmers 36 cents to pass through.

Now, you have more trivia questions to impress your friends. - LCG

---

[59] https://en.wikipedia.org/wiki/Panama_Canal (accessed 6/17/18)

Thought for Today (November 16)

THE "INTERESTING FACTS" DEPARTMENT

Thanks to evidence of fermented beverages derived from rice found at a 9,000-year-old site in China's Henan Province, we've known for a while that the ancient Chinese enjoyed a drink. However, in 2016, we learned that the Chinese were also beer lovers. Archaeologists excavating the Shaanxi Province found beer-making equipment dating to 3400–2900 BCE.[60]

This marks the first direct evidence of beer being made on-site in China. Residue found in the vessels also revealed the ingredients of the ancient beer, including broomcorn millet, lily, barley, and a grain called Job's tears.

The presence of barley was surprising especially because it pushed back the arrival of the crop in China by 1,000 years. According to current evidence, the ancient Chinese used barley for beer centuries before using it for food.

Beer before food . . . well, we know the ancient Chinese had their priorities right. - LCG

---

[60] https://www.thevintagenews.com/2017/02/14/oldest-beer-making-factory-found-near-the-wei-river-in-china/ (accessed 6/17/18)

Thought for Today (November 17)

THE "YOU SHOULD RUN FOR OFFICE" DEPARTMENT

"As an economist, I'm assuming that you're assuming the same thing that I'm assuming." - Lorelei St. James

---

. . . as a non-economist, I'm assuming that you have assumed the correct assumption. - LCG

Thought for Today (November 18)

THE "GROWING OLD GRACEFULLY" DEPARTMENT

"I don't plan to grow old gracefully. I plan to have face-lifts until my ears meet." - Rita Rudner

---

. . . and, could that make wearing earrings a problem? - LCG

Thought for Today (November 19)

THE "CALL IT FINANCIAL RELIEF" DEPARTMENT

Although it may be hard to believe, a number of colleges and universities are naming restrooms after people who make large donations. For example, the Harvard Law School now has a restroom named after an alumnus.

William Falik, a Harvard Law School graduate, donated $100,000 to his alma mater—and Wasserstein Hall now has the "Falik Men's Room." [61]

Other universities, such as (among others) Philadelphia's University of Pennsylvania and the University of Colorado at Boulder, are making money off of their restrooms.

At Penn, for example, the donor requested plaques on restroom walls that state, "The relief you are now experiencing is made possible by a gift from Michael Zinman." [62]

. . . I guess this is one way you can [begins with "P"; rhymes with "Hiss"] away your money! - LCG

[61] www.dailycal.org/2012/02/06/mens-room-named-after-uc-berkeley-professor-falik/ (accessed 6/17/18)

[62] https://www.chronicle.com/article/Their-Research-Is-in-the/239583 (accessed 6/17/18)

Thought for Today (November 20)

THE "ALOHA" DEPARTMENT

AUTHOR'S NOTE: My wife and I lived in Hawaii for nearly 10 years; therefore, I have decided to provide . . .

A Brief History of Hawaii

The history of Hawaii, known as "The Aloha State," goes back many centuries. The first settlers, Polynesians from the Marquesas Islands, set foot on Hawaii Island (the southernmost island known as "The Big Island"), approximately 1,500 years ago.

500 years later, Polynesian settlers from Tahiti arrived. The Tahitians brought with them beliefs in gods and demi-gods and instituted a strict social hierarchy based on a kapu (taboo) system.

Over the centuries, Hawaiian culture flourished, and it was during this period that the iconic Hawaiian arts of hula and surfing were embraced. Unfortunately, there was some trouble in paradise: land division conflicts between ruling *ali'i*, or chieftains, were common.

In 1778, Captain James Cook landed at Waimea Bay on Kauai, which is the most northern of the major Hawaiian islands. Naming the archipelago the "Sandwich Islands" in honor of the Earl of Sandwich (his financial benefactor), Cook opened the doors to the west. Cook was killed a year later in a fight with Hawaiians in Kealakekua Bay on the Big Island.

In 1791, aided by cannon from an English merchantman, Chief Kamehameha united the warring factions of the Big Island and embarked on a campaign to conquer (or "unify") all of the Hawaiian Islands. Fierce battles were fought on Maui and Oahu, resulting in the deaths of thousands of warriors. However, by 1810, Kamehameha succeeded in uniting Hawaii into one royal kingdom.

In 1819, less than a year after King Kamehameha's death, his son, Liholiho, abolished the ancient kapu system. In 1820, the first Protestant missionaries arrived on the Big Island, bringing with them Christianity,[63] which filled the void left by the demise of the kapu system. They brought also western diseases,[64] which took a heavy toll on the Native Hawaiian population.

Western influence continued to grow and, eventually, American Colonists controlled much of Hawaii's economy. In 1893, the Colonists, with the help of the American military, overthrew (stole) the Hawaiian Kingdom in a peaceful, but controversial coup. In 1898, Hawaii became a territory of the United States.

In the late 19th and early 20th centuries, sugar and pineapple plantations fueled Hawaii's economy. The

---

[63] The missionaries banned hula and surfing, believing them to be scandalous and sacrilegious. As a result, these "arts" were practiced clandestinely by the Hawaiians until they became accepted again in the early 20th century.

[64] To this day, influenza is known (colloquially) as the "American Disease" in many Pacific islands.

island of Lanai, under the leadership of James Dole, became the world's leading exporter of pineapple and was known as the "Pineapple Island." Meanwhile, on all the islands, the labor-intensive production of pineapple and sugar cane required plantation owners to recruit Chinese, Filipino, and Portuguese immigrants to fill the "labor void." This mix of immigrant ethnicities is what makes Hawaii's population so diverse today.

On December 7, 1941, the Japanese launched a surprise attack on Pearl Harbor on Oahu. Four years later, on September 2, 1945, Japan signed an unconditional surrender on the battleship USS Missouri, which rests in Pearl Harbor today.

In 1959, after decades of unsuccessful petitioning, Hawaii became the 50th State of the United States.

Aloha, Hawai'i - LCG

Thought for Today (November 21)

THE "CLASSICAL QUOTES" DEPARTMENT

"All men are guilty of the good deeds they did not do."

- Voltaire

Francois-Marie Arouet (21 November 1694 - 30 May 1778) is better known by his pen name, "Voltaire." - LCG

Thought for Today (November 22)

THE "WONDERFUL WORDS OF WISDOM" DEPARTMENT

"And so, my fellow Americans, ask not what your country can do for you—ask what you can do for your country."

- John Fitzgerald Kennedy

John Fitzgerald "Jack" Kennedy (May 29, 1917 - November 22, 1963), commonly referred to by his initials JFK, was an American politician who served as the 35th President of the United States from January 1961 until his assassination on November 22, 1963. - LCG

Thought for Today (November 23)

THE "WORDS OF WISDUMB" DEPARTMENT

You think no one cares if you're alive?

Try missing a car payment.

. . . it works! I got mail and my phone never stopped ringing! - LCG

Thought for Today (November 24)

THE "THANKSGIVING HOLIDAY" DEPARTMENT

AUTHOR'S NOTE: Since Thanksgiving falls on the fourth Thursday in November, it is hard to pin the holiday to a specific date. Therefore, I selected arbitrarily November 24. - LCG

Thanksgiving

Thanksgiving falls under a category of "harvest" festivals that spans cultures, continents, and millennia.[65] After the fall harvest, the Egyptians, Greeks, and Romans feasted and paid tribute to their gods. Thanksgiving resembles the ancient Jewish harvest festival of Sukkot. And Native Americans commemorated the fall harvest with feasting and merrymaking long before Europeans set foot on the continent.

However, Americans have been taught that Thanksgiving began with the Pilgrims who left England on the Mayflower in September 1620. They established a colony in Plymouth, Massachusetts after a harsh 66-day crossing of the Atlantic; and they suffered a brutal first winter in which one-half of the Mayflower's passengers died. During that first winter, the settlers forged an alliance with a local tribe, the Wampanoag.[66]

---

[65] https://en.wikipedia.org/wiki/Thanksgiving (accessed 6/177/18)

[66] It was an alliance that would endure for more than 50 years and, tragically, remains one of the few examples of harmony between European colonists and Native Americans.

In November 1621, after the Pilgrims' first corn harvest proved successful, Governor William Bradford organized a celebratory feast and invited the Wampanoag chief Massasoit. The festival lasted for three days and is remembered now as America's "first Thanksgiving"—although the Pilgrims themselves did not use the term at the time.

The "Thanksgiving" tradition grew: The Pilgrims held a second Thanksgiving celebration in 1623 to mark the end of a long drought, the Continental Congress designated days of thanksgiving during the American Revolution, and in 1789, George Washington issued the first Thanksgiving proclamation by the national government. John Adams and James Madison designated days of thanks during their presidencies also.

In 1817, New York became the first of several states to adopt officially an annual Thanksgiving holiday; however, each state celebrated the holiday on a different day, and the American South remained largely unfamiliar with the tradition. In 1863, at the height of the Civil War, Abraham Lincoln issued a proclamation that scheduled Thanksgiving for the final Thursday in November. And finally, in 1941, President Roosevelt signed a bill making Thanksgiving the fourth Thursday in November.

"There is one day that is ours. Thanksgiving Day is the one day that is purely American." - O. Henry

"Vegetables are a must on a diet. I suggest carrot cake, zucchini bread, and pumpkin pie." - Jim Davis

Thought for Today (November 25)

THE "THOUGHTS ON THANKSGIVING" DEPARTMENT

"As we express our gratitude, we must never forget that the highest appreciation is not to utter words, but to live by them." - John Fitzgerald Kennedy

----

I give thanks for all that I have: for the failures I have overcome, the forgiveness I have received, the triumphs I have experienced, and the people I have helped and who helped me in return. There is so much more; and for all, I give thanks. - LCG

Thought for Today (November 26)

THE "EVERY GIRL'S DREAM" DEPARTMENT

"Every guy thinks that every girl's dream is to find the perfect guy. Please . . . every girl's dream is to eat without getting fat." - Every Girl

----

"Spandex is a privilege, not a right." - Dave Thomas

Thought for Today (November 27)

THE "WORDS OF WISDUMB" DEPARTMENT

Procrastinate now! Don't wait to hesitate!

- Lawrence C. Gambone

. . . thought that one up myself; but, procrastinated—I waited quite a while before I hesitated to add it to this book. - LCG

Thought for Today (November 28)

THE "SIGN OF THE TIMES" DEPARTMENT

A real measure of wealth would be how much you are worth if you lost all of your money.

. . . Ah, since I haven't got any money, I'm worth very little whether I lose it or not. – LCG

Thought for Today (November 29)

THE "MEASURE OF SUCCESS" DEPARTMENT

"Behind every successful man you'll find a woman who has nothing to wear." - Harold Coffin

"Behind every successful man is a surprised woman."
- Maryon Pearson

"Behind every successful man is a woman. Behind her is his wife." - Groucho Marx

"Behind every successful man is a woman who didn't marry me." - Al Bundy

"Behind every successful man stands a surprised mother-in-law." - Voltaire

"Behind every successful man there's a lot of unsuccessful years." - Bob Brown

---

. . . and behind every "unsuccessful" man is a woman who will never let him forget it. - LCG

Thought for Today (November 30)

THE "CELEBRITY BIRTHDAY" DEPARTMENT

Samuel Langhorne Clemens

Samuel Langhorne Clemens (November 30, 1835 - April 21, 1910), better known by his pen name Mark Twain, was an American writer, entrepreneur, publisher and lecturer.[67]

Samuel Langhorne Clemens was a major American writer from Missouri. He wrote 28 books and numerous short stories, letters, and sketches. His stories and novels are famous for their humor, vivid details, and memorable characters. Twain's first book, "The Innocents Abroad," was published in 1869. His best-known works are "The Adventures of Tom Sawyer" (published 1876) and "The Adventures of Huckleberry Finn" (published 1885), both classics in American literature.

At 17, Clemens left Hannibal, Missouri for a printer's job in St. Louis. In 1858, while still in St. Louis, Clemens became a licensed river pilot. Clemens' pseudonym, Mark Twain, comes from his days as a river pilot. "Mark twain" is a river term utilized on a boat when sounding the depth of water. It means two fathoms or 12-feet, a depth safe to navigate.

---

[67] https://en.wikipedia.org/wiki/Mark_Twain (accessed 6/17/18)

Quotes by Mark Twain

Whenever you find yourself on the side of the majority, it is time to pause and reflect.

If you tell the truth, you don't have to remember anything.

Don't go around saying the world owes you a living. The world owes you nothing. It was here first.

The secret of getting ahead is getting started.

Go to Heaven for the climate, Hell for the company.

Kindness is the language which the deaf can hear and the blind can see.

It is better to keep your mouth closed and let people think you are a fool than to open it and remove all doubt.

Do the right thing. It will gratify some people and astonish the rest.

All generalizations are false, including this one.

Giving up smoking is the easiest thing in the world. I know, because I've done it thousands of times.

. . . I would add a little known fact here, but I don't know one. - LCG

DECEMBER

December

December is the twelfth and final month of the year in the Julian and Gregorian Calendars and is the seventh and last of seven months to have a length of 31 days.

December got its name from the Latin word *decem* (meaning ten) because it was originally the tenth month of the year in the old Roman calendar, which began in March. In the early days of Rome, the winter days following December were "monthless;" they were not included as part of any month.

When the months of January and February were created out of the monthless period and added to the beginning of the calendar, December moved from the tenth to the twelfth month, but retained its name.

Thought for Today (December 1)

THE "THIS WILL GIVE YOU GAS" DEPARTMENT

The First Drive-in Gas Station

The first "drive-in" filling station, designed specifically to sell fuels and other related products, was opened to the motoring public by Gulf Refining Company in Pittsburgh, Pennsylvania on December 1, 1913.[68] This was the first architect-designed station and the first to distribute free road maps.

A plaque has been erected on the site. The plaque reads:

> *At this site in Dec. 1913, Gulf Refining Co. opened the first drive-in facility designed and built to provide gasoline, oils, and lubricants to the motoring public.*

On its first day of business the station sold 30 gallons of gas at 27 cents per gallon.

There is a claim that the world's first "purpose-built" gas station was constructed in St. Louis, Missouri in 1905, and the second gas station was constructed in 1907 by Standard Oil of California (now Chevron) in Seattle, Washington. But, these early stations did not have drive-up fuel pumps—shopkeepers filled a five-gallon can from behind the store and brought it to the customer's car.

According to the Pennsylvania Historical and Museum Commission:

---

[68] http://www.post-gazette.com/business/2013/12/01/FILL-ER-UP/stories/201312010079 (accessed 6/17/18)

Prior to the construction of the first Gulf station in Pittsburgh and the countless filling stations that followed throughout the United States, automobile drivers pulled into almost any old general or hardware store, or even blacksmith shops in order to fill up their tanks.

You know, I'm thinking that 27 cents per gallon in 1913 sounds pretty expensive to me. - LCG

Thought for Today (December 2)

THE "YOU READ IT ON THE ROAD" DEPARTMENT

BUMPER STICKERS:

BRAIN CELLS COME AND BRAIN CELLS GO

. . . FAT CELLS LIVE FOREVER!

BRAINS May Have the Plans . . . .

But **STUPID** Has All the Good Stories.

. . . Brain cells die and are gone forever; fat cells reproduce. - LCG

Thought for Today (December 3)

THE "LESSONS ON LIFE" DEPARTMENT

"I think men who have a pierced ear are better prepared for marriage. They've experienced pain and bought jewelry." - Rita Rudner

---

"Marriage is a wonderful invention . . . then again so is a puncture repair kit." - Billy Connolly

Thought for Today (December 4)

THE "WAY OF THE WORLD" DEPARTMENT

When I was young and thin, I wore tight-fitting clothes. Now, I'm old and fat; and I wear tight-fitting clothes.

> - L. C. Gambone

. . . to paraphrase Aldous Huxley (see the March 16 Thought for Today), nothing is different; but everything has changed. - LCG

Thought for Today (December 5)

THE "DOG DOGMA" DEPARTMENT

"Don't accept your dog's admiration as conclusive evidence that you are wonderful." - Ann Landers

---

. . . however, you can accept your cat's disdain as conclusive proof that you are inconsequential. - LCG

Thought for Today (December 6)

THE "INFLATION AFFECTS US ALL" DEPARTMENT

"My dog is worried about the economy because Alpo is up to $3.00 a can. That's almost $21.00 in dog money."

- Joe Weinstein

My dog is fat . . . which means I'm not getting enough exercise. - LCG

Thought for Today (December 7)

THE "DAY OF INFAMY" DEPARTMENT

All Americans are familiar with President Franklin D. Roosevelt's emotionally charged address to Congress on December 8, 1941:

"Yesterday, December 7, 1941—a date which will live in infamy—the United States of America was suddenly and deliberately attacked by naval and air forces of the Empire of Japan."

What is not so well known is that there is no record of Japanese Admiral Isoroku Yamamoto having said the famous words (attributed to him), "We have awakened a sleeping giant and filled him with a terrible resolve."

However, after attacking Pearl Harbor on December 7, 1941, Admiral Yamamoto did make a prediction about the outcome of the coming naval war with the United States.

"I can run wild for six months," Yamamoto said, ". . . after that, I have no expectation of success."

Before the onset of hostilities, Admiral Isoroku Yamamoto voiced his opposition to war with the United States, believing it to be a war that Japan could not win. As it happened, the Battle of Midway, the critical naval battle considered to be the turning point of the war in the Pacific, ended with a decisive American victory on June 7, 1942, exactly six months after the Pearl Harbor attack. - LCG

Thought for Today (December 8)

THE "STUFF YOU NEVER THOUGHT ABOUT" DEPARTMENT

Why Friday is called . . . well, uh . . . Friday

The name Friday comes from the Old English *Frīgedæg*, meaning the "day of Frige," a result of an old convention associating the Old English goddess Frigg with the Roman goddess Venus, with whom the day is associated in many different cultures. The same holds for *Freitag* in Modern German, and *vrijdag* in Dutch.

In modern Swedish, Norwegian, and Danish, the name for Friday is *Fredag,* meaning Freyja's day. The distinction between Freyja and Frigg in some Germanic mythologies is contested.

Friday is associated in many cultures with the goddess Venus and the planet named for her. The word for Friday in most Romance languages is derived from the Latin *dies Veneris* or "day of Venus." Examples are: *vendredi* in French, *venerdi* in Italian, and *viernes* in Spanish.

An exception is Portuguese, also a Romance language, which uses the word *sexta-feira*, meaning "sixth day of liturgical celebration," derived from the Latin *feria sexta* used in religious texts where it was not allowed to consecrate days to pagan gods.

Friday is liberation day; it signifies the "end" of the work week. - LCG

Thought for Today (December 9)

THE "CONSPIRACY COMPLEX" DEPARTMENT

Are you paranoid if it **IS** as bad as you think . . . and they **ARE** out to get you?

. . . Quick . . . where can I hide? - LCG

Thought for Today (December 10)

THE "CULINARY COST-CONSCIOUSNESS" DEPARTMENT

"Food is too expensive. Last night I went to a $100 a plate dinner in my own kitchen." - Chris Cassatt

---

. . . I won't be impressed with technology until we can download food and booze. - LCG

Thought for Today (December 11)

THE "DOG DOGMA" DEPARTMENT

"I wonder if other dogs think poodles are members of a weird religious cult." - Rita Rudner

---

I always wondered why they did that to those poor dogs. - LCG

Thought for Today (December 12)

THE "PROFESSED PROFESSIONALISM" DEPARTMENT

THE TEST OF THE PROFESSIONAL

This is the "Test of the Professional."[69] Its four questions are designed to stimulate your creative thinking processes; so try to resolve the questions without reading the answers provided . . . . Ah, go ahead! . . . Read the answers right away! It's what I did! - LCG

1. How do you put a giraffe into a refrigerator?

The Correct answer is: Open the refrigerator, put in the giraffe, and close the door.

[This question tests whether you tend to do simple things in an overly complicated way.]

2. How do you put an elephant into a refrigerator?

Answer: Open the refrigerator, put in the elephant, and close the refrigerator.

Well . . . actually that is the wrong Answer! The Correct Answer is: Open the refrigerator, take out the giraffe, put in the elephant, and close the door.

[This tests your ability to think through the repercussions of your previous actions.]

---

[69] www.smart-jokes.org/giraffe-refrigerator-elephant.html (accessed 6/17/18)

3. The Lion Pride is hosting an animal conference. All the animals attend except one. Which animal does not attend?

Correct Answer: The Elephant. The elephant is in the refrigerator.

[This tests your memory.]

OK, even if you did not answer the first three questions correctly, you have one more chance still to show your true abilities.

4. There is a river you must cross, but it is inhabited by crocodiles; there is no bridge and you do not have a boat. How do you manage it?

Correct Answer: You swim across. All the crocodiles are attending the Animal Conference.

[This tests whether you readily comprehend what you read as well as learn quickly from your mistakes.]

According to research consultants, 90% of the professionals tested got all questions wrong. But many preschoolers got several correct answers. This disproves conclusively the theory that most professionals have the brains of a four year old.

. . . but, it proves conclusively the theory that, in theory, theories, once theorized, can be tested theoretically. - LCG

Thought for Today (December 13)

THE "TEE'D OFF" DEPARTMENT

"Give me fresh air, a beautiful partner, and a nice round of golf . . . and you can keep the fresh air and the round of golf." - Jack Benny

"It took me seventeen years to get 3000 hits in baseball. I did it in one afternoon on the golf course."- Hank Aaron

"I know I'm getting better at golf because I'm hitting fewer spectators." - Gerald Ford

"Although golf was originally restricted to wealthy, overweight Protestants, today it's open to anybody who owns hideous clothing." - Dave Barry

"Golf was invented by people who think music comes out of a bagpipe." - Dean Martin

---

"It looketh like a silly game."
                    - King James IV (upon banning golf in 1491)

Thought for Today (December 14)

THE "POET LAUREATE" DEPARTMENT

"The world is full of willing people; some willing to work, the others willing to let them." - Robert Frost

----

Here's an OLDFART test: You are a bona fide "oldfart" if you remember the TV character Maynard G. Krebs and understand the significance of his less-than-immortal words, "Work? WORK!" - LCG

Thought for Today (December 15)

THE "YOU LEARNED IT FROM LCG" DEPARTMENT

The scientific name for a football-shaped object is "Prolate Spheroid."

. . . Which is why my high school had an "Erudite Cheer:" Deter them! Deter them! Induce them to relinquish the prolate spheroid! - LCG

Thought for Today (December 16)

THE "SUMMING UP HUMAN NATURE" DEPARTMENT

"Human action can be modified to some extent, but human nature cannot be changed." - Abraham Lincoln

"Everyone is as God made him, and often a good deal worse." - Miguel de Cervantes

"It is easier to denature plutonium than to denature the evil spirit of man." - Albert Einstein

"Nature does not deceive us; it is we who deceive ourselves." - Jean-Jacques Rousseau

"It is human nature to think wisely and act in an absurd fashion." - Anatole France

"Never underestimate the human capacity for delusion."
                                            - Roger Cohen

"Man - a reasoning rather than a reasonable animal."
                                            - Alexander Hamilton

Thought for Today (December 17)

THE "CLASSICAL COMMENTS" DEPARTMENT

"Human subtlety will never devise an invention more beautiful, more simple or more direct than does nature because in her inventions nothing is lacking, and nothing is superfluous." - Leonardo da Vinci

---

I wonder, Leonardo, does "beautiful" include nature's cockroaches and mosquitos? - LCG

Thought for Today (December 18)

THE "WHAT'S IN A NAME" DEPARTMENT

Michelangelo's Full Name:

Michelangelo di Lodovico Buonarroti Simoni

I'm not sure, but I think Michelangelo is famous for saying to the Pope, "You want WHAT on the ceiling?" - LCG

Thought for Today (December 19)

THE "WRIGHT IS NEVER WRONG" DEPARTMENT

"I'm having amnesia and déjà vu at the same time. I think I've forgotten this before." - Steven Wright

---

Me, too; just like the last time, I've forgotten what to say here. - LCG

Thought for Today (December 20)

THE "STUFF YOU NEVER THOUGHT ABOUT" DEPARTMENT

Why Saturday is Called . . . Saturday

Saturday is named after the Roman god and planet Saturn and is the only day of the week that retained its Roman origin in English. Sometime in the 2nd century CE, the Romans named Saturday *Sāturni diēs* ("Saturn's Day") for the planet Saturn. It was also around this time (by the end of the 3rd century) that the Romans adopted the seven-day week.

Between the 1st and 3rd centuries CE, the Roman Empire gradually replaced the eight-day Roman *nundinal*[70] cycle with the seven-day week. The Roman authors Vettius Valens and Dio Cassius (and the medieval English author Geoffrey Chaucer in his *Treatise on the Astrolabe*) explained the astrological order of the days. According to these authors, it was a principle of astrology that the heavenly bodies presided, in succession, over the hours of the day. The association of the weekdays with the

---

[70] Borrowed most likely from the Etruscans, the *nundinal* cycle, market week, or 8-day week (Latin: *nundinum* or *internundinum*) was the cycle of days marked using *nundinal* letters from A to H. The earliest form of the Roman calendar included 38 such cycles, running for 304 days from March to December followed by an unorganized expanse of 50 winter days. The lengths of the Republican and Julian calendars, however, were not evenly divisible by 8; under these systems, the *nundinae* fell on a different letter each year.

respective deities is thus indirect, the days are named for the planets, which were in turn named for the deities.

The Germanic peoples adapted the system introduced by the Romans, but supplanted the Roman deities with their indigenous gods in a process known as *interpretatio germanica*.[71] This held true for all the week days except Saturday, for which the Roman name was adopted directly by West Germanic peoples—apparently none of the Germanic gods were considered to be counterparts of the Roman god Saturn.

To me, Saturday is a good day, because it isn't part of the normal "Work Week." - LCG

---

[71] *Interpretatio germanica* is the practice by the Germanic peoples of identifying Roman gods with the names of Germanic deities. This occurred around the 1st century CE, when both cultures came into closer contact.

Thought for Today (December 21)

THE "LISTEN TO THE MUSIC" DEPARTMENT

"A composer is a guy who goes around forcing his will on unsuspecting air molecules, often with the assistance of unsuspecting musicians." - Frank Zappa

Frank Vincent Zappa (December 21, 1940 – December 4, 1993)[72] was an American musician, composer, activist and filmmaker. His work is characterized by nonconformity, free-form improvisation, sound experiments, musical virtuosity, and satire of American culture.

In a career spanning more than 30 years, Zappa composed rock, pop, jazz, jazz fusion, orchestral, and musique concrète works. He produced almost all of the 60-plus albums that he released with his band the *Mothers of Invention* and as a solo artist. Also, Zappa directed feature-length films and music videos, and designed album covers. He is considered one of the most innovative and stylistically diverse rock musicians of his era.

"All the good music has already been written by people with wigs and stuff." - Frank Zappa

---

[72] https://en.wikipedia.org/wiki/Frank_Zappa (accessed 6/17/18)

Thought for Today (December 22)

THE "WORDS TO LIVE BY . . . OR NOT" DEPARTMENT

"If at first you don't succeed, then I would advise you, most definitely, to avoid skydiving." – Anonymous

---

. . . Yeah, and maybe cliff jumping, alligator wrestling, bomb disposing, prize fighting, test piloting, tightrope walking, lion taming, trapeze swinging, bull riding, shark baiting, arguing with your wife . . . . - LCG

Thought for Today (December 23)

THE "EDUCATION IS THE KEY" DEPARTMENT

"Your whole life has been training for right now."

- Robert Asprin

. . . most of us probably need re-training. - LCG

Thought for Today (December 24)

THE "RURAL WISDOM" DEPARTMENT

AUTHOR'S NOTE: Many would say that there is no better advice than the simple, heartfelt, down-to-earth sayings from the wise old folks in rural America.   So, here's a handful of country wisdom straight from Grandma's front porch. - LCG

Forgive your enemies . . . . It messes up their heads.

Hard work pays off in the future . . . . Laziness pays off now!

Keep skunks, lawyers, and bankers at a distance.

Letting a cat out of a bag is whole lot easier than putting it back.

Never argue with a fool . . . an impartial witness won't be able to tell the difference.

There is no such thing as a free puppy.

Success is merely a matter of luck . . . . Just ask any failure.

Never back anything into a corner that's meaner than you.

When you are in it up to your eyeballs, keep your mouth shut.

"Anger" is just one letter short of "Danger."

Never try to explain what you don't understand.

A dog has so many friends because he wags his tail instead of his tongue.

To get something you never had, you have to do something you never did.

Treat each day as if it were your last . . . . One day you'll be right.

Yep, practical advice from America's heartland . . . pulled from the internet, no less . . . . I'll bet you were expecting some sort of Christmas Eve type of thing here, weren't you (with, you know, Santa Claus, Christmas Carols, elves, and stuff)? - LCG

Thought for Today (December 25)

THE "HOLIDAY GREETING" DEPARTMENT

For this special day I'll just keep it simple and wish all Christians a Very Merry Christmas. For those of you who are not Christian, I wish a very happy holiday season.

- Lawrence C. Gambone

Yep . . . A HAPPY HOLIDAY TO ALL! - LCG

Thought for Today (December 26)

THE "IRONY OF LIFE" DEPARTMENT

"By the time you've gained enough knowledge and experience to know your way around, you find out that you're too old to go anywhere." - Unknown

----

. . . Too old and too broke . . . . . - LCG

Thought for Today (December 27)

THE "POLITICAL POLEMICS" DEPARTMENT

"The ideal form of government is democracy tempered with assassination." - Voltaire (1694-1778)

Voltaire . . . a man ahead of his time. - LCG

Thought for Today (December 28)

THE "SCIENTIFIC SUPPOSITIONS" DEPARTMENT

"The scientific theory I like is that Saturn's rings are composed entirely of lost airline luggage." - Mark Russell

----

So that's where my stuff went? - LCG

Thought for Today (December 29)

THE "DEFINING DEMOCRACY" DEPARTMENT

"Democracy is two wolves and a lamb deciding what to have for dinner." - Benjamin Franklin

"The great thing about democracy is that it gives every voter a chance to do something stupid." - Art Spander

"Democracy: You consent to having your pocket picked, and elect the best man to do it." - Benjamin Lichtenberg

"Democracy is a device that ensures we shall be governed no better than we deserve." - George Bernard Shaw

---

I still think "Despomockeracy" is the most appropriate term. - LCG

Thought for Today (December 30)

THE "MAN'S BEST FRIEND" DEPARTMENT

Dogs were man's best friend 7,000 years ago according to evidence found at Blick Mead near Stonehenge.[73] Archaeologist David Jacques found a dog's tooth that belonged to an animal originally from an area known today as the Vale of York.

The dog served as a companion to a Mesolithic hunter-gatherer. The two undertook a 400 kilometer (250 mile) trip from York to Wiltshire, which is now considered the oldest known journey in British history. Jacques argued that the dog was domesticated, part of a human tribe, and most likely used for hunting.

Durham University later confirmed his findings through isotope analysis performed on the tooth enamel. It showed that the dog drank from water in the Vale of York area. They also believe that the dog would have looked similar to a modern Alsatian with wolf-like features.

Dogs have owners . . . cats have staff. - LCG

---

[73] https://www.theguardian.com/science/2016/oct/07/archaelogists-evidence-earliest-known-journey-uk-history-stonehenge-wilsthire-mesolithic-man-dog (accessed 6/17/18)

Thought for Today (December 31)

THE "NEXT TIME" DEPARTMENT

December 31 — This is the only day of the year when "next day," "next week," "next month," and "next year" are interchangeable.

– L. C. Gambone

New Year Resolutions You Actually Can Keep!

Skip more classes in school.
Call in sick at work more.
Go shopping more often.
Eat more unhealthy food (like fries and burgers).
Drink more soda instead of fruit juice.
Exercise less. Sleep more.
Work less. Watch TV more.

So, Happy New Year . . . and, I'll get back to you next millennium. - LCG

Lawrence C. Gambone

BONUS

LEAP YEAR
THOUGHT FOR TODAY

BONUS
Leap Year Thought for Today
(February 29)

THE "NOT NECESSARILY COMPREHENSIVE NOR DEFINITIVELY CORRECT" DEPARTMENT

Disclaimer: Except where noted, all statements and opinions within this thesis are purely those of the author, who, nevertheless, not only refuses to accept responsibility for anything written, but also reserves the right to disclaim, retract, or disavow any expressed or implied statement or opinion.

GAMBONE'S GRATUITOUS GUIDE TO COMPARATIVE ENGLISH

English is not a monolithic language; it contains enumerable divergences of expression, inflection, pronunciation, spelling, grammar, and meaning that go beyond the mere dissimilarities of regional colloquialisms. I find this fascinating. Therefore, I have contemplated the "English" of the world's three major English-speaking countries, England, the United States (includes Canada, a wholly owned subsidiary), and Australia; and I have come up with the following determinations:

ENGLAND (British English or King's English) — British English includes England only because, according to British scholars, the fact that English actually is spoken in Ireland, Scotland, and Wales has not been confirmed. British English may sound colorful to the untrained ear, but it is the most boring English of the English-speaking nations. This is because British English, although it does have some peculiar vernacular, for the most part is staid, stolid, and mired in a mundane colloquial background.

British English is the most sanctimonious version of the language, however, because its speakers believe that British English is the true King's English. They are incorrect, of course: Since 1066, the true King's English has been French—prior to that it was German.[74]

THE UNITED STATES (American) — American English is referred to disdainfully by the other two nations as "American" as in, "You don't speak English; you speak American!" By far it is the most emphatic English. American will bounce off the other versions of English (and even non-English languages), and then turn around to roll over them, making them American. Thus, American can accept such vernacular as, "donnybrook" and "billabong," "rendezvous" (from French), and "dollar" (from the German "thaler") without even batting an eye.

American is also the most definitive English (judged by the fact that it is the foundation for nearly all technical terms and computer jargon); and probably has the highest percentage of bad (or "four-letter") words in everyday household usage than any other language.

AUSTRALIA (Australian) — To this day, there is doubt among etymologists whether or not Australian is actually English. Aside from a rather loose sentence structure and diverse rules of grammar, Australian employs words

[74] . . . and prior to that it was Latin; and prior to that it was Celtic . . . .

that aren't even words; for example: "dinkum," "dunny," "chook," and "jumbuck." This distinctive idiosyncrasy has some relation, no doubt, to the fact that Australia is situated in a different hemisphere, supremely distant from its other English-speaking cohorts.

Speakers of American love Australian, believing it to be "colorful" (it has something to do with the inflection). However, speakers of the King's English will go to great lengths to ensure their English is not compared to—nor mistaken for—such an "indecorous form of prosaic linguistics."

But, it goes without saying, any language that has 40 definitions for toilet in its dictionary (with about 120 things you can do in it) goes w-a-a-a-y beyond being "colorful."

Thus: Comparative English according to Gambone, whose ancestral language, of course, is Italian. (Please see the disclaimer.)

"Great Britain and the United States are nations separated by a common language." - George Bernard Shaw (1856-1950)

"We have really everything in common with America nowadays except, of course, language." - Oscar Wilde (1854-1900)

"Me fail English? That unpossible!" - Ralph Wiggum

I disclaim everything except the disclaimer. - LCG

Lawrence C. Gambone

ABOUT THIS BOOK . . . .

For a number of years, I forwarded emails to friends and associates that contained various "Thoughts for Today;" and for the most part, (occasional death threats and pending lawsuit notifications notwithstanding) these emails were well received. Many recipients replied to me with positive comments that, in effect, said, "I hope you are keeping these to put in a book;" and "You should write a book."

In response to such encouragement, I decided to compile my individual emails and add some new material, culled with painstaking effort from the internet, to develop a book. The result is this compendium.

The bibliography for this book is simple. Nearly everything was garnered from the internet, exceptions being the quips and quotes that I attribute modestly to myself, and the occasional fascinating fact or story forwarded to me by friends. On the internet, Wikipedia, BrainyQuote, and other websites were major sources of information. The source locations have been footnoted throughout the text.

While I did take efforts to ensure that my information was correct, I must inform the reader that fact checking was minimal or, in many cases, nearly non-existent. In essence, for the purposes of this book, if the internet says it is so; then so it is (and we all recognize the internet's viability as an "impeccable" source of reliable information).

As a result, I do not claim to be an authority on anything presented within this book; nor do I intend this book to be used as a reference. Thus, any resemblance to a true fact or any departure from fiction may or may not be purely coincidental.

If, while reading this compendium, you happen to discern a fact or figure that is incorrect; you may wish to point this out to the author, who, of course, is me. I can assure you that your effort will be appreciated. Nevertheless, my decided response will be to shrug my shoulders, offer to you (silently) a rousing "good catch;" and ignore your rejoinder from that point on.

- Lawrence C. Gambone

Lawrence C. Gambone

ABOUT THE AUTHOR

Lawrence Gambone lives in an apartment building that has a grand view of the building next door. He has no money, no talent, no valuable possessions, and no mistress. However, he does have a wife (which is why he has no money), a large stereo system, a cacophonous collection of CD's, a beat-up guitar, a monstrous amplifier, a neurotic dog, and a car that burns regular gas. He used to have a neurotic bird; but the dog ate it.

Assessing Gambone's personality is difficult indeed, since most people who know him would point out, rather adamantly, that he doesn't have one. Nevertheless, by stretching all levels of credibility, the following can be derived:

Politically, Gambone is left of right. Sociologically, it would be right if he left. Psychologically, he is w-a-a-a-y off center. Nevertheless, Gambone works hard. And when he plays, he plays loose. But, unfortunately, when he tries to think . . . he falls asleep.

Made in the USA
Middletown, DE
05 September 2023

37650404R00179